photographing your product

norbert nelson

photographing your product

for advertising & promotion

a handbook for designers & craftsmen

VNR VAN NOSTRAND REINHOLD COMPANY
NEW YORK   CINCINNATI   TORONTO   LONDON   MELBOURNE

Van Nostrand Reinhold Company Regional Offices:
New York   Cincinnati   Chicago   Millbrae   Dallas

Van Nostrand Reinhold Company International Offices:
London   Toronto   Melbourne

Copyright © 1970 by Litton Educational Publishing, Inc.
Library of Congress Catalog Card Number 71-128613

Designed by Jean Callan King
Line drawings by Patrick S. Kennedy
Printed by Halliday Lithograph Corporation
Color printed by Bridge Lithographic Co., Inc.
Bound by Haddon Bindery

Published by Van Nostrand Reinhold Company
450 West 33rd Street, New York, N.Y. 10001

Published simultaneously in Canada by
Van Nostrand Reinhold Company Ltd.

16 15 14 13 12 11 10 9 8 7 6 5 4 3 2 1

CONTENTS

Introduction

Those who are involved in some form of the visual arts are inclined to look on photography primarily as an art medium. That is, they do when they are conscious that an image is photographic or, perhaps, consciously artistic. A news picture, photographs in a mail-order catalog, or the reproduction of a painting are also photographs. In such cases, the purpose of the photograph or the message it conveys is the important element, and we are likely to overlook the fact that we are looking at a photograph at all. If the message communicated by a commercial photograph or photographic process is so quickly accepted that we do not think about the means through which we received the message, chances are that the photograph is a good one and its reproduction adequate.

This text concerns itself with photography as a multifaceted tool for those who are, in one way or another, engaged in the creation or presentation of objects. Photography will be presented here as a means of communication rather than as an artistic end in itself. This book presents techniques and tools which, if employed properly, will allow the creative worker to communicate visual ideas easily. Its aim is to provide the reader with an introduction to basic photographic tools and methods which will help him to sell, publicize, record, and advertise products, and to transmit visual ideas — over distances or in face-to-face meetings.

A mastery of the rudiments of photograph-making offers the "creator of things" another means of communicating his ideas as represented in his creations. We all learn to talk or write about the things we do as a matter of course. Unfortunately, most of us must learn the techniques of visual communication at a later date.

The practice of photography is so broad and varied that no one text can hope to do more than isolate one area of photography and explore it. The surgeon thinks of photography in terms of X rays, the printer in terms of reproduction; to the banker a camera is a device augmenting his security system. Since the artist, craftsman, industrial designer, manufacturer, and perhaps the merchant, for whom this book is written, are primarily concerned with physical objects in their working life, this book concerns itself with the photography of such objects — with still-life, or product, photography.

It is my admittedly prejudiced point of view that it is with still-life photography that serious involvement in picture making should start. Many photographers start in a more popular area of photographic concentration — recording the scene as they find it. They take their camera to their subjects, while I bring things to my camera to create a subject. The demands of still-life photography go well beyond this commonplace observation. I can control almost every element of the picture I make in a studio setup, whereas they have to work with what they find. I can manipulate light and shadow, length of exposure, depth of focus, accentuation of texture, the tonality of what is before my lens. They cannot. My work is slow. I can spend upwards of thirty minutes on one of a series of catalog photographs, and hours on a more difficult shot. I am forced to examine each element which contributes to the picture I am making: light, scale of objects, distortion, highlights, and the many factors which enter into mood. They think of *taking* a picture rather than *making* a picture. Having been forced to examine each element of my picture, when I do go out to *take* pictures, I believe I see more critically because of my studio disciplines.

The mastery of the techniques of still-life photography can provide a sound basis for other photographic activities. The photographic journalist, if he is good, has long since mastered the basic techniques of making pictures. He must work so rapidly that he makes technical judgments almost subconsciously. A developed ability in any interpretive photography also rests on sound photographic practice and a knowledge of technique, but in still-life work the subject is not going to go away. You have time to study your subject and try variations on your basic approach.

The making of photographs of your own work cannot usually be delegated satisfactorily, especially if you are seriously involved with the work you have done. By making your own photographs, you avoid a loss "in translation." The hack photographer will probably not capture what you see in an object, and the creative photographer is likely to inject something which was not there in the first place. It is almost easier, unless you have a great and steady volume of photographic work to be done, to learn to do it yourself rather than to train someone else to do it your way. It is a lot cheaper to do it yourself and often a great deal more convenient, and it is always more fun to see your own work turn out well. Perhaps, too, you never look at an object so critically as when it is "under the lights."

It should be stated here at the outset that I am not a professional photographer. From time to time over the past twenty-five years I have, often for reasons of economic convenience if not necessity, turned to photography as a means of making money and have found it a remunerative skill. I did find, however, that the more involved I became with photography as a busi-

8

ness, the less I was able to enjoy it as a serious avocation. I am currently well along toward recapturing my amateur standing. This presentation, then, is made from a serious amateur point of view. The approach has many advantages for the reader. The professional who is involved every working hour with photography takes for granted many of the basic problems which the occasional photographer encounters. Basics have become habit for the professional. He has mastered and uses many sophisticated techniques and processes which may have required a great deal of study and experimentation to perfect. His equipment and tools are necessarily quite varied and super-capable. He has probably made an investment in equipment which is beyond the practical means of even serious amateurs. The commercial photographer must prepare himself and his tools to handle almost anything that comes through the studio door. Chances are that you will have a particular type of photographic problem to master in connection with your work, not a host of widely varied problems. Concentration of effort and investment in equipment can, therefore, be limited to your immediate needs at any given moment. The equipment, techniques, and processes discussed herein are limited to those which are within the reasonable grasp and financial reach of almost any serious worker.

Finally, I must give the reader warning that this book will not concern itself with the rudiments of operating a camera or learning to read an exposure meter. Many basic texts which will impart this elementary information are available — free with the equipment you buy, or for a dollar or two in photography supply stores, or in the public library. The material contained herein presupposes that you are or will become familiar with the operation of your camera, have placed it on a tripod, and want to learn to make photographs of products or other objects. Since there is practically no limit to the amount of useful knowledge a serious photographer can acquire, I have included at the end of the book a bibliography to carry the ambitious worker beyond the scope of this book. My selections of additional reading may appear eclectic, but they are useful texts that I have found to be especially helpful.

Technical Note

Unless otherwise noted, all illustrations in this book were photographed using a $2^1/_4''$ x $3^1/_4''$ Linhof Technica with a 120 roll-film adapter. All exposures were standardized on Kodak Plus-X film and developed in amateur roll-film tanks using Kodak D-76 developer diluted 1:1 at recommended temperatures. All exposures were made according to meter readings. In most instances an incident light meter was used, but certain materials, such as glass, required the use of a reflected-light meter.

Prints were enlarged under amateur darkroom conditions using an Omega enlarger and the camera's Symmar lens.

When the location has a message, you have to go outside to shoot your subject. This photograph was made to announce, in a trade advertisement, the arrival of a new collection of imported home furnishings. In the actual advertisement, the background of the ship and sheds was toned down by airbrush retouching, leaving the merchandise clear in the foreground. The camera was a 4″ x 5″ Linhof with a standard 6″ lens, and a fill-in flash, close to the camera, was used.

1.The Use of the Photograph

The use to which you will put the photographs you make determines the type of end product you need. Photographs can be presented as prints or slides, in color or black-and-white. Prints will vary in size according to their intended use. Texture, visual quality, and the mechanics of presentation depend on where and how the pictures will be seen. In other words, the photographer must know what he wants to do with the pictures he makes before he makes them. The end product necessarily determines, to a great extent, the photographer's choice of materials, equipment, and working technique. To master the whole range of photography, or even the broad spectrum of product photography, is the work of a lifetime. To learn to make the specific kind of photographs you need in your work can be far less demanding and, once mastered, can provide the art- or design-oriented professional with a convenient and economical means of visual communication. Some of the most common uses for photography in the worlds of art and design are: as a teaching tool and for group presentations; as a publicity and public relations tool; for use in catalogs and other printed material; as a selling tool (the salesman's photograph); as a means of recording your own work and that of others; as a means of selling your talents (the photographic portfolio); and as an element in exhibits.

While most photographs can be produced and reproduced in a number of forms, we shall examine the most commonly required "end products" as a guide.

SLIDES FOR TEACHING OR GROUP PRESENTATION

The classroom and the business meeting room present similar problems for the exhibit of photographs. In both cases your visual and/or verbal message must reach a number of people simultaneously. Where a group of more than four or five people is involved, the logical means is a projected image: a transparency or slide.

The viewing conditions you set up depend to some extent on your objective. Do you wish to use slides as a stimulus to discussion or to deliver a complete message without interruption? If you want to use slides as a part of an ongoing discussion, you will want some light in the room. This will enable you to see those with whom you are working and allow them to see you. You can introduce other elements, such as demonstration models, into the discussion without a radical change in the viewing atmosphere. If the projected image is not required to be too large, projection can be satisfactorily carried out in a dim, but not dark, interior. The size of the screen and the amount of ambient light present determine the power of the projection unit you need. Another possibility for viewing in near-normal light is the rear-projection screen, where a bright image is shown through a viewing surface.

If you wish to work without interruption from the beginning of your presentation to the end, darken the room. We are conditioned, through years of movie going, to be quiet when the lights go out. The projected image also appears brighter in a darkened room.

The 35 mm. slide has become almost universally accepted for projection purposes. Almost grainless films, ready-mounted transparencies, and a wide variety of projection equipment have all enhanced the convenience of using this size. You can be certain almost any organization will have a suitable slide projector for 35 mm. transparencies.

At present, one can see on the horizon a great resurgence of the $2^{1}/_{4}''$-square reflex camera. These are also excellent slidemakers; better, in fact, than most 35 mm. cameras. The very fact that you start with a transparency more than three times as large as the 35 mm. slide insures far better quality of detail. There are many projectors available for $2^{3}/_{4}'' \times 2^{3}/_{4}''$ mounted slides, and most processors will return them in cardboard mounts, just as they do with 35 mm. slides. Such projectors are not so frequently found as the 35 mm. kind, and you may often find yourself carrying a projector to the meeting or classroom. But if you are going to be working in black-and-white and color prints as well as slides, this larger-size camera has a great deal to recommend it.

To show slides to one or two people, you can also use simple viewers or table projection units which carry their own changers and small screens. Mini-projectors, which take up little room in a briefcase, and very sophisticated units, some of which offer automatic changing, focusing, slide-retrieval and storage systems, sound synchronization, multi-projector synchronizing rigs, and other features, are also available.

There are also projectors for showing prints, but their slowness of operation, large size, and lack of projection quality makes them less practical than slide projectors.

Slide shows have much in common with movies in that there is, or should be, a presentation designed to explore and drive home a particular point or idea. Unless the slides are simply a cataloging of individual elements, there must be a consideration of timing and pace, with peaks and valleys of visual and dramatic interest. The show should be sketched out just as a shooting script would be prepared for a cinematic creation. This is often best done by developing a script on paper outlining what you want to say and then tagging in the slide changes at appropriate spots in your presentation. Slides must be prearranged in a meaningful sequence which builds to a logical conclusion or totality. Even if there is to be no commentary with the slides, an appropriate recorded musical background will frequently enhance the effectiveness of a slide show.

A verbal presentation with a slide show may be either live or recorded. This is largely a matter of personal choice. If you speak easily and know just what you want to say, you have the advantage, in a live presentation, of being able to change your speech in response to the reaction of your audience. In selling, a live sales pitch with slides is undoubtedly preferable to a "canned" one. Tape recordings, on the other hand, have the advantage of having been prepared, polished, and timed in advance. A simple audible cue, such as a beep or a buzzer, indicates when to change slides. Sound-slide synchronizers are commercially available at reasonable cost.

THE PUBLICITY PHOTOGRAPH

A publicity photograph almost never stands on its own; rather it illustrates a written text in the form of a caption or a press release. The photograph must therefore be closely related to the text furnished to an editor. Its secondary function is to arrest attention so that the text will be read, and, when used in this fashion, it should, perhaps, be more provocative and visually exciting than when the picture is self-explanatory.

If you look at any newspaper, it is apparent that people are most interested in people. Most news illustrations and feature stories in popular magazines concern themselves with what people are doing, have done, or are about to do. While this is not the only kind of publicity photograph possible, the publicity shot containing a human figure is likely to elicit more interest from the publications to which it is sent. Such pictures necessarily depart from the realm of pure product photography with which this text is concerned, but most of us are quite used to taking pictures of people, and the general rules that apply to good product photographs will cover a product-plus-person picture. In thinking about using people in pictures, it is not necessary to use a whole figure. If you are photographing a wine glass, for

example, a hand would be sufficient. A silver earring may require only a partial side view of a properly coiffed head.

When using a live model, even if he is a close friend or a member of the same business organization in which you are employed, it is well to have an executed model-release form on file. Such a release, signed by the model, gives you the right to use the picture in which he appears for commercial purposes. Standard model-release forms are available in professional photographic supply houses and are frequently advertised in photography magazines. The few pennies for the form and the minute it takes to complete one and file it in a folder can protect you from a lawsuit. One general model-release form is included in an appendix to this volume.

A second kind of publicity photograph shows an object in use or in its proper setting. A lamp, for example, usually would be far more interesting to a home-fashions editor when photographed in a partial room setting than when shown against a no-seam paper background. A crafted leather belt can be effectively shown as a part of a fashion ensemble.

People are fascinated with seeing things being made. The noses poked in fence holes around a construction site or the gaggle of onlookers in front of a pizza-parlor window attest to the universality of this very human trait. It follows that pictures of products in the process of design or fabrication will attract attention, especially if the story has to do with the unique aspects of a product's manufacture.

Finally, a photograph might well show an element of product differentiation. The photograph should then illustrate what makes the product unique. When Polaroid came out with a camera that signaled when the print was ready, their photographs in the trade magazines focused on the camera's audible timer. A new razor featuring adjustability will be released with publicity pictures showing the adjustment mechanism.

Having made a photograph to illustrate your message, there is the question of what type of photographic print to send to the publication. In the area of newspaper publicity, the 8″ x 10″ glossy print is standard. Glossy photographs are produced more quickly and consequently more cheaply, at quantity-print houses.

Publicity photographs are often needed in quantity to mail to several publications simultaneously. In the case of pictures for newspaper reproduction, you must provide prints geared to the lowest common denominator of printing. Newsprint is not the best paper for recording detail or nuances

Opposite:
Publicity photographs showing people engaged in unusual activities are often of interest. This photograph of master potter and designer Fong Chow was exposed by multiple flash: three #5 bulbs in studio reflectors. One illuminates the background, a second is placed high to the left of the camera, and a third is on the camera, with Kleenex tissues used as a diffuser. The camera was a 9 x 12 cm. Linhof with a 6″ Tessar lens.

of tone; coarse screens are more the rule than the exception in preparing prints for newspaper reproduction. A print with strong highlights and solid masses of tone, in other words, a somewhat contrasty print, will fare better in this medium than a superbly detailed study with subtle tonal nuances.

If your target is a slick magazine, perhaps an art or design publication which prides itself on graphic quality, a fine photograph, well printed, is in order. The better magazines usually prefer to make their own pictures and may well ask to borrow the object to be illustrated. When a publication wants to reproduce your product in color, it will almost invariably request that the product be photographed by its own photographer. The cost of color reproduction is so high and so technically demanding that the expense of making a special photograph to the magazine's own standards is minor when viewed as part of the total cost. Color transparencies sent to editors should therefore have as their sole purpose the introduction and explanation of some features of your work. You can always offer to furnish color photographs to their specifications after they express interest.

The publicity photograph is so closely tied to the written message that it is necessary to touch, at least briefly, on the material which should accompany the photograph when it is sent to an editor. First, the purpose of publicity should be clearly understood. Only an amateur will settle for the satisfaction of seeing his name or work in print. Publicity is a selling tool which should be used to bring your product or service compellingly to the attention of potential buyers or to enhance its value in the marketplace. Timing is important. Used prematurely, before you are ready to deliver what you are selling, it can do little more than breed dissatisfaction.

Because you do not pay for the space or time in which publicity releases appear, they seem to have been selected as newsworthy. The reader seldom realizes that newspaper or magazine editors and producers of television shows are always hungry for interesting material. When you are publicized, the authority of the publication or medium which selected you or your work for presentation acts to reinforce your own reputation. In this sense, publicity carries more authority than paid advertising. An accumulation of publicity clippings can be an excellent sales or presentation tool.

The basic written form for presenting your material to an editor is the press release. A press release may be printed in its totality or in part. Always add to the end of a release the line: "For further information contact: name, address, and phone number." Press releases vary widely in content and somewhat in format, but a few fairly constant characteristics would include:

a heading: "Press Release."
from: a statement as to who is releasing the information.
release date: a time after which all editors may release the information.
    (Editors respect release dates. You cannot break faith by releasing information to one of two competitive publications while holding the other to a release date.)

brevity: printed space costs money! The editor is looking for ideas and information clearly and concisely presented in crisp, short sentences. He is not seeking a literary masterpiece.

the "V" shape: every release should be written with the idea that it will be cut. Put the most important facts and thoughts at the beginning of the release. Information of less immediate or general interest should follow with the most important point always preceding less vital information. The bottom of the release is where the blue pencil marks are likely to be found.

If you are mailing your releases and photographs to more than one magazine in a field of interest or to more than one newspaper in a city, the text released to each of the different publications should differ to some degree, illustrative material should be clearly different. Exclusivity is expected by competing editors even when it is not specifically requested.

THE CATALOG OR ADVERTISEMENT PHOTOGRAPH

The catalog or advertisement photograph is a selling tool in its purest form. While it is generally accompanied by description and/or specifications, such a picture should provide several types of information almost simultaneously in order to attract sufficient interest for the copy to be read and studied. These include: a clear visual description of the item with the object's most salient or unique qualities highlighted; an indication of the object's use; and, possibly, some indication of the object's size. This scale can be clearly established by the inclusion of some common item, such as a recognizable coin next to a bank, an apple in a bowl, a pair of spectacles on a cocktail table, a pencil resting near a geographic globe, a cigarette near an ashtray.

The technical demands made on a black-and-white or color catalog photograph are stringent, and allowances must be made for loss of detail in the printing process. (These factors are discussed more fully in Chapter 11, "Preparing for the Printer.")

To photograph a collection of similar items for use in a catalog, you can use size for emphasis and develop interest through page layout as well as in the individual pictures. If one object is similar to, but visually more interesting or commercially more important than others in the group, it might be photographed against an interesting background with carefully planned accessory detail and lighting. Photographs of other items in the same group should be smaller and purely descriptive. In fact, if one photograph serves to explain one of a collection of items fully, and the other objects that are to be shown with it vary only in shape, or perhaps in accessory elements or size, you might use line drawings, which are cheaper to print than halftones, in combination with the one photograph to explain the group.

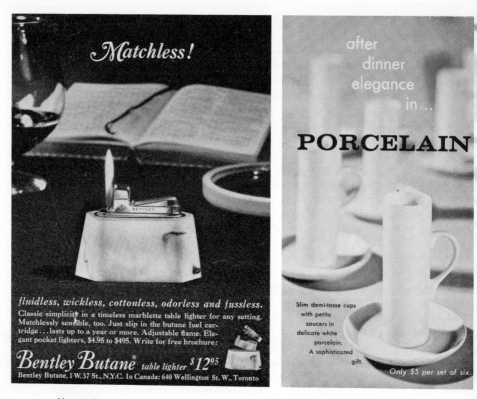

Above left:
Advertising must make a specific statement with photographs. In the Bentley Butane advertisement, the object is to set a mood of elegant ease for a new fashion lighter. The brandy
snifter, book, and ashtray are intended to suggest relaxation. Note the use of selective
focus to subdue the background object. Camera was a 9 x 12 cm. Linhof Technika with a 6″
Tessar Lens.

Above right:
The use of selective focus creates a repetitive background design for the china demitasse
cups in the foreground.

    Black-and-white photographs for catalog use should be printed on
matte paper for convenient retouching. Such pictures are often used in sil-
houette. This means that the background is eliminated through retouching
before the picture is printed. Obviously the retoucher will have an easier
time with an object originally shot against a bright white background or a
light box. Good separation of tone between the object and the background
will substantially reduce the need for retouching. Lighting that crisply picks
up important detail will make it unnecessary to highlight detail through
retouching.

THE SALESMAN'S PHOTOGRAPH

A selling photograph presents essentially the same problem as the catalog photograph. In the hands of a salesman, agent, or gallery representative, such a photograph will lessen the need for a detailed description. Your picture must concern itself with setting a mood and illustrating the quality of the object shown. The salesman is there to offer specific information and to describe more fully that which requires description.

At the very least, a good selling-print should: (1) clearly show what you are selling; (2) be of sufficient quality to tell the prospect how you feel about what you are offering him; (3) unify your group of objects or ideas either through similarity of selection or mode of presentation; (4) create excitement. Salesmen usually carry many presentations or many groups to show their customers. Your photographs should be packaged in such a fashion that they will be impressive and easily distinguished by both salesman and customer. Furthermore, they should be large enough to be seen by all the people involved in making the buying decision. A salesman offering a product is likely to confront only a single buyer or purchasing agent, and, perhaps, a representative of management. In such cases an 8" x 10" photograph is sufficiently large. An offering to the board of directors of a gallery or museum shop would involve a large group, in which case the smallest acceptable print would be 11" x 14".

Salesmen's photographs should be sturdy, either on double-weight paper, well mounted, or perhaps bound in plastic. They should not, however, be so burdensome to carry or handle that the man acting for you will find them difficult to use. As a general rule they should not be bound in a permanent order. The sales process generally requires comparison, selection, and discussion. Single photographs can most easily be manipulated to a given end by the person making the presentation. (Inability to manipulate individual slides is one of the principal deterrents to using them for product sales work.)

A salesman's print will also often require a written description. It differs from the catalog description in that it provides pure information, not selling copy. When you present a product through a salesman, the descriptive information attached to it should include: (1) an identifying number or letter code for the item; (2) the name of the object; (3) the sizes and/or capacities of the objects illustrated, and perhaps of similar objects not shown; (4) a material description and the full specifications of the objects illustrated; (5) color descriptions and variations (in addition to any samples or color photographs you may include); (6) notes on packaging; and (7) the price, or other basis for determining cost of a product.

The descriptive information should be permanently affixed to the photograph. While information is sometimes printed photographically on the face of the photograph (a service most quantity-print houses offer at very low cost), I feel that words detract from the image. A typed, Xeroxed, or mimeo-

graphed sheet attached to the back of the photograph is generally more satisfactory.

The use of a transparency for face-to-face selling situations is seldom
satisfactory. Difficulty in manipulation, the need for special viewing equipment, and the cost of duplicating transparencies all indicate the use of
prints. Both color and black-and-white prints are discussed in detail in following chapters.

RECORDING YOUR OWN WORK

Memories tend to fade very quickly. A photographic record of your work
can provide you with a tool for self-criticism, a record of earlier ideas, a
catalog for insurance purposes, a record for customers, a file of techniques,
and a base on which to create presentations for special commissions. In its
simplest form such a record may consist of snapshots classified in albums
designed to accept a single size of commercial print or in a file box with
indexed card separators. If you do not anticipate a need for reproducing
your photographs from negatives, Polaroid pictures can provide an excellent record. If your eventual aim is group presentation, slides in slide boxes
might well be the easiest answer. Negatives can be filed with prints but
should first be put in glassine envelopes to keep them clean and prevent
abrasion.

If it is important to keep the pictures over a period of several years,
black-and-white prints, well fixed and thoroughly washed to remove the acid
fixer, will outlast color slides. The lasting qualities of both will depend on
their being stored under dry, relatively cool conditions.

When establishing a record-keeping system it is important to pick one
method and stick to it. Photographs made for other purposes may be used
for this, but since the purposes for which they are made may demand prints
or transparencies of different types and sizes, it is wise to make an extra
print or slide specifically for your record.

THE PHOTOGRAPHIC PORTFOLIO

A photographic portfolio of work can be an informal collection of pictures
of your work or a collection of photographs, interestingly mounted and creatively presented, which approach art in themselves. Photographs for a portfolio are, in essence, selling pictures. They do not sell a product, but rather
a range of capability. They must communicate, without words, a great deal
about you: how you feel about the things you have done and your aesthetic
viewpoint.

The method of presentation must be as artistically exciting as the con-
tents of your portfolio. Having looked at innumerable designers' work over

he years, I believe I remember the presentations more vividly than what they contained. There are no rules or limits for such portfolios. The best have the same visual variety as a good magazine spread. There is variation in photograph size. Color may be used descriptively on a page beside a black-and-white photograph that sets the mood. Toned prints are acceptable. Line drawings, actual designs, even blueprints used graphically may help establish an idea. They may be pressed on mounting board, on backgrounds of burlap, or metallic Mylar. A portfolio may be compactly designed in a semibound fashion or may simply be a container to hold sheets that can be set up as an instant exhibition.

In a portfolio it is the dramatic effect, the visual impact, and the creativity visible in presentation that count rather than any conformity to standard patterns. When you hear a photographer say that he is shooting for his portfolio, he generally means that he is making some rather "far out" pictures that he knows no client or agency art director is likely to use but which will make a visual impact the prospect will remember. Scope and excitement are his aims and should be yours.

Most art and photographic supply stores sell either photographic mounting boards or more flexible white cover stock for mounting photographs. The use of photographic mounting tissues provides a clean and convenient method of mounting your photographs. The tissues are available in standard photographic-paper sizes, and are inexpensive and easy to use. A tissue is placed between the back of the photograph and the surface on which the photograph is to be mounted. The layers are then pressed together, under heat, in a photograph-mounting press, or with a dry, hot iron.

Rubber cement is, of course, an old standby; and, for permanent mounting, I have found that Elmer's Glue-all and similar products work well. When using liquid cements, weight the photographs under a board to insure that they dry flat and adhere completely. Sandwiching the picture between thin pieces of foam, felt, or blanket material will help to equalize pressure. A sheet of waxed paper between one print and the next will prevent unwanted adherence. Mounting two photographs on the same board, back to back, eliminates some possibility of the board warping.

PHOTOGRAPHS FOR EXHIBITION

Photographs used in exhibit work are as varied in their size, form, subject matter, and purpose as the exhibits of which they are a part. Photographs may form an exhibit in themselves but they are more frequently used to supplement an exhibit of objects. They are often used when the subject they illustrate cannot itself be brought into the exhibition. At their best, photographs add an extra dimension to the objects on exhibition. An exhibit of handicraft objects might be supplemented by photographs of the remote places in which they were made or by pictures of the craftsmen making the objects. An architect might display models but supplement them by the use of photographs of details of his finished work. A designer of large farm equipment or power-generating plants could not bring more than a few objects to even a large show. Pictures of on-site installations would supplement the few products and models on display.

Photographs can be used to illustrate the use of exhibited material. An artist working in ceramic mural techniques might bring one or two large murals for exhibition; but he would necessarily rely on pictures to show how they have been used in the interiors or exteriors of buildings. Pictures can be used to establish a historical background or reference points for contemporary work. The communication possibilities of photographs on exhibition are almost endless.

Exhibition prints are generally large. Such photographs may be 16″ x 20″ or may cover a wall.

While you might be able to handle a 16″ x 20″ in a well-equipped normal darkroom using a top-quality enlarger and improvising big trays from aluminum foil pans or whatever, making big prints presents processing problems. Even the professional studio sends exhibition prints to professional laboratories which specialize in this type of work. If the laboratory you use does not make large exhibition prints, it will be able to refer you to one that does.

The technical demands made on your negatives are extreme in exhibition-print work. Using even a 2″ x 3″ negative and utilizing almost the full format, you are blowing up the area about a hundred times to reach a normal 20″ x 30″ exhibition print. Even allowing for the fact that people view large prints from a greater distance than small ones, detail is diluted in the extreme. A large negative, top-quality optics, fine-grain film, and the best processing techniques are all required to produce top results.

The black-and-white print is expensive to produce in sizes over 16″ x 20″. The cost of color prints becomes astronomical. If you need color in your exhibition, consider the projection of slides. Properly projected, these can give you large images and, with relative simple automatic changing mechanisms, can project a series of images. If you do not possess an automatic projector, such machines, complete with changing devices, can be rented from photographic dealers in larger cities. A powerful projector, preferably 1000 watts, can be placed in a moderately lighted room to project on an opaque reflecting wall or screen or through a translucent rear-projection screen. Most automatic equipment uses 35 mm. slides.

Having led you to a consideration of the photographic end toward which you are working, let us now consider the means of accomplishing it.

2. The Black-and-White Print

The black-and-white print is, with the possible exception of the 35 mm. slide, the least expensive kind of photographic end product. Certainly if a number of prints of a subject are required, prints are far more economical than slides, unless the multiple slides are made in the camera. If cost is the prime determinant, then black-and-white prints should usually be the choice.

There are two basic ways to make a print: contact printing and projection printing (enlarging). In contact printing the negative is placed in contact with the print paper by means of a print box or frame which holds both negative and paper flat under pressure. A light is shined through the negative onto the paper.

Contact printing is unsurpassed for quality of image, and the very critical workers who demand absolute perfection in prints often use large negatives that permit large finished contact prints. They generally use an 8″ x 10″ camera. For occasional use, such a large studio camera would prove burdensome. Lenses and film are expensive, and the processing of such negatives in a home darkroom, even a good one, requires much space, large quantities of solutions, and either big handling equipment or the time-consuming alternative of processing one sheet at a time in a tray. But if you are a perfectionist by nature, use an 8″ x 10″ view camera. There is nothing smaller that will match its quality.

Most of us see contact prints as proof prints or sheets. Contact proofs for negatives 2¼″ square or larger can easily be viewed without gadgets and provide a quick and easy way to pick the best negative of a series or to preview negatives before enlarging. If you have a 4″ x 5″ camera, a 4″ x 5″ contact print can be used for record keeping, in portfolios, and even for reproduction in many cases.

Most of us who are less than full-time professionals use equipment to make a 4″ x 5″ or smaller negative. Daylight developing tanks for 4″ x 5″ and smaller sizes are inexpensive and easy to use, making it possible at least to process your own film, even if you do not want to get into the complications of a darkroom and printing setup. Film is cheap enough to use freely, as you must in experimentation and for critical work.

From any given negative, the apparent quality of the resulting print will vary inversely with size. Apparent quality is also a function of viewing distance. The farther you are from a print, the more detailed it appears. As a practical matter, a print should be large enough to enable the viewer to see all the important features and details of the picture comfortably. In black-and-white film the 8″ x 10″ print is generally acceptable. However, for portfolio work you may wish to emphasize certain subjects with larger prints and make others less important by including smaller prints. I would suggest 3¼″ x 4¼″ to be the smallest workable print. Smaller black-and-white prints are just too hard to see.

Once you have a good black-and-white negative, you can begin to work with it. Size can be varied through enlargement. In enlarging, unwanted material can be cropped by filling the printing paper with the portion of the image desired. You can accentuate or reduce elements within the picture area by holding back the light in part of a picture (dodging) or giving some part of a picture additional exposure during printing (burning in). Many professional laboratories will give you a chart of standardized symbols to help you instruct them how to use these techniques on your work and will work with you in manipulating a print to achieve a desired effect. A chart of symbols for instructing the laboratory is included in an appendix.

Contrast can be varied considerably from the same negative to achieve prints for different purposes. Let us assume you want to use the same negative to make a large print for exhibition and a number of prints to be sent to newspapers. With black-and-white film, you can make your exhibition print on a large sheet of photographic paper of a texture suitable to your subject and print for a wide range of full tones from clean white to deep rich blacks. The publicity prints should be somewhat more contrasty. They can be printed on a harder paper to eliminate many of the intermediate gray tones which might appear muddy in newspaper reproductions.

The dramatic effect of a photograph can also be changed in printing. A straight shot will attempt to show best range and detail in the subject itself. To establish a lighter, more delicate mood, you might want to make a print of higher key. A light print could be made printing only for the darker details and washing out the middle tones. If this is intended, however, at the time of shooting all background and unessential elements should be kept light in color or white. A low-key, or more dramatic, photograph will be produced if dark tones predominate, perhaps with edges burned in.

Even the color of the blacks in black-and-white photography can easily be altered in the black-and-white print by use of certain papers and chemical toners. Some papers are warm toned, tending toward brown-blacks, and others cold toned, ranging toward blue-blacks, when used with proper developers, and more accentuated hues in an extended range of tones can be obtained with toning solutions. While it is likely that such devices would be resorted to only for exhibition prints, there is no reason not to consider them for portfolio or even sales presentations in black-and-white. One nice thing about toning is that it can be experimented with after the prints are made, even after they are dry.

RETOUCHING

Retouching is a technique that, except in the most sophisticated photographic laboratories, is limited to black-and-white photography. Often when shooting a picture, and more frequently after you have exposed and developed a negative, you wish you had eliminated a highlight or defined a subject better. What you did not do with lights and camera, you can sometimes do with pencil, airbrush, or retouching tools. Even skilled retouchers do not like to work on negatives smaller than 4″ x 5″, and they prefer negatives even larger. If you are shooting subjects where retouching must be considered, it is sensible to expose larger negatives. Retouching can often save a marginal negative and make an adequate negative better. Retouching can also be done on prints, but when several prints are required, it means work on each individual print.

QUANTITY PRINTS

In black-and-white or color, unless the quantity of copies needed exceeds a hundred, the direct photographic print will not only prove most economical, but it is certainly the best-quality medium. Once you have the negative, there is little or no preparation cost for making most prints, and the price of each print will probably drop as the quantity ordered increases. When you need many prints, seek out a photographic laboratory that specializes in quantity prints.

Black-and-white enlargements are likely to cost three to ten times as much as contact prints. If you need only a few prints, the cost of enlargements probably will not be prohibitive. If you need ten or more enlarged black-and-white prints of a given subject, a black-and-white copy negative may be the answer. Have a laboratory make a first-class black-and-white print from your negative, then have a negative made from the good print. The copy negative can be 5″ x 7″ or 8″ x 10″. With a large negative, contact prints of the subject can be made quickly and cheaply. It must be said that in going through the extra step of a copy negative, there is some loss of tonal gradation and overall quality. Prints from copy negatives tend to be more contrasty. However, if handled by a competent professional, the results can be reasonably successful for most subjects.

BLACK-AND-WHITE FILM CHARACTERISTICS

The kind of black-and-white prints you need should determine your choice of film. In examining the various film characteristics, you can go as far into the technicalities of photography as you choose. For those of a technical bent, there are several good publications dealing with films listed in the bibliography. For the moment, let us limit ourselves to a few of the fundamental considerations.

Film Speed. This is a minor consideration in still-life photography unless you are working with such limited lighting equipment as to make very long exposures necessary. Convenience generally dictates a shutter-timed exposure of a second or less, but by using a cable-release setting, with your shutter on "time" or "bulb," and mounting your camera on a steady tripod, you should have no problem in making time exposures of several seconds.

Graininess. This is caused by the clumping of the silver grains which form the black image on a negative. Grain tends to increase with film speed, but today, unless an unusually high degree of enlargement is required, as is the case with large exhibition prints, grain is not a serious problem with medium-speed films which are correctly exposed and carefully developed. Improper development of black-and-white film can create more grain problems than the selection of the wrong film. Overdevelopment can be a real villain, as can overexposure, since graininess is more noticeable when printing a dense negative than when a normally exposed or even slightly thin negative is used.

When your films are processed commercially, you should specify fine-grain development. This is a service offered by any good laboratory, and it is especially important if you are using a small negative. With a 35 mm. negative, fine-grain film and processing are essential. If you are processing your own films, use the fine-grain developing formula recommended by the manufacturer and read the instructions carefully. Some combinations of film and fine-grain developer actually slow down your film and require an increase in exposure. Check the developing notes packed with your film before exposing it.

Most important, when you find a film-developer combination that pleases you, use it consistently. You will thereby reduce the number of variables which can affect the quality of the images you produce.

Resolving Power. This is the capacity of a film to record fine detail so that it can be clearly seen. While technically this is measured in lines per millimeter, you will be concerned with seeing the details of the subject you are photographing clearly and distinctly. When necessary details can no longer be distinguished and degenerate into a gray mass, you have lost a practical degee of resolving power. Over- or underexposed negatives kill a film's resolving power and destroy that wonderful brilliance which characterizes a really good print.

26

The quality of the lens you use also affects the resolving power of a film. The lens should be able to resolve at least three times as much detail as the film to give you full resolution in a negative. Let us assume a film of medium resolving power can record clearly 90 lines per millimeter; your lens should be able to handle at least 270 lines per millimeter. Such a lens would be pressed when your camera was loaded with film of extremely high resolving power (225 lines per millimeter). Again, in practical terms, any good-quality lens stopped down two or three stops below its maximum aperture should be adequate. A cheap lens, especially on a small camera, will be a constant frustration.

Often the film or lens is blamed for the more frequent fault of camera movement during exposure. The photographer working on a wood floor who moves during a two-second exposure is more likely to destroy detail through the vibrations from his movement than through the choice of the wrong film or lens. A stiff cable release which moves the camera during exposure, the vibration of a machine, such as an air conditioner, or certain types of focal-plane shutters which set up vibrations when they open can also destroy resolution.

To hold sharpness with a camera whose shutter does set up vibrations when released on a "time" or "bulb" setting, carry an oversize black lens cap (a round jar top with the inside painted matte black will do as well) and use it to cover the lens before and after a long exposure. Open the shutter (raise the mirror on a single-lens reflex) while holding the cap over the camera lens. Move the cap a fraction of an inch away from the lens and hold it there until you are sure any vibration caused by the removal of the cap has stopped. Then remove the cap entirely from in front of the lens for the period of exposure, recapping it at the end of the exposure, and closing the shutter while the lens is capped. Although impractical for exposures of less than a second, this is a highly convenient way to insure against vibrations when shooting still-life photographs with exposure times of several seconds.

Acutance. More frequently referred to as sharpness, acutance is actually the ability of a film to record a sharply defined division between two elements in the same scene. Let us assume a black line of great sharpness on a white sheet of paper. When you photograph it, the light from the white area tends to spill over onto the almost-clear portion of the negative representing the black line. This results from the diffusion of light within the light-sensitive emulsion layer of the film itself. Modern films with thin emulsion coatings are readily available and, if considerable enlargement is anticipated, it is best to choose a film with the ability to reproduce great sharpness.

Definition. All three factors—resolving power, graininess, and acutance — interact to produce an image of good or poor definition. Definition is the impression of crisp, clear images that we all work for as photographers. If a film is badly exposed or processed and is excessively grainy, image clarity falls off long before the limits of resolution or acutance are reached. It does not matter how good a lens you have on your camera. The photographer generally falls short long before his equipment or materials reach their limits, so here are a few questions to use as a checklist for yourself when your results are less than perfect: (1) Is the lens clean? (2) Did you focus carefully? Use a magnifier to view your ground glass if you feel uncertain. (3) Did the camera move? If you are shooting without the aid of a tripod—inexcusable in still-life work except in emergencies—keep your shutter speed at 1/100 of a second or faster! (4) Do you have a dense negative as a result of overexposure (check your meter or reduce your exposure next time) or overdevelopment? (5) If all the above check out as properly handled, your enlarger (or someone else's enlarger) may be the problem. Is it rock steady? Was it properly focused? Double check the focus if your work is done on an autofocus-type enlarger.

There are a great number of fine foreign and domestic films available; it would be impossible to discuss them all here. I am therefore limiting my examples to the films of Eastman Kodak, which are readily available and which dominate our market in the United States. In so doing, I do not wish to imply that the products of Ansco (GAF), DuPont, Perutz, Agfa-Gevaert, Ilford, and other fine manufacturers are any less satisfactory. Do, however, avoid unbranded and out-of-date film bargains.

Kodak, in a recent publication (1967), lists over twenty different black-and-white roll films alone. The choice of Kodak sheet films is even greater. Many of these are special-purpose films, of course, for copying, infrared work, black-and-white slides, portraiture, and other particular situations. Many of these have little or no application to still-life photography. Kodak films which would be reasonable choices for still-life work would certainly include the following:*

Film	Graininess	Resolving Power	Acutance
Verichrome This old standby is a great film. It will tolerate a lot of exposure error and still produce a negative of good quality.	Extremely Fine	Very High	Very High
Plus-X Pan My personal choice for an all-around film. Its tonal gradation is excellent and can be altered considerably in development.	Extremely Fine	High	Very High

Film	Graininess	Resolving Power	Acutance
Panatomic-X	Extremely Fine	Very High	Extremely High

This is the film to pick if you know your negatives will have to be greatly enlarged. With a 2¹/₄″ square negative, developed in Microdol X or a similar fine-grain formula, you can make blowups almost without limit. Its contrast characteristics are somewhat flatter than Plus-X, in my experience, but are still excellent. At an A.S.A. speed rating of 32, it is about one-fourth as fast as Verichrome or Plus-X. But, when you are on a tripod in the studio, who cares?

Film	Graininess	Resolving Power	Acutance
Tri-X Pan	Very Fine	Medium	Very High

This film is on the high-speed end of the general purpose roll-film range. It is about twelve times as fast as Pan-X and three times as fast as Plus-X. It can be enlarged greatly with good definition but not to the extent of its slower cousins. If you find a subject where you need great depth of field — where you must stop your lens down until it is quite slow — and may at the same time have to stop some motion (shooting a mobile sculpture could be such a problem) you will find this film a good choice.

Try a few different black-and-white films in combination with some of the recommended developers to see which results you personally prefer. Then, for similar subjects, standardize!

*Technical specifications from *Kodak Black and White Films in Rolls*. Similar and additional data on Kodak Sheet Films is available in *Negative Making with Kodak Black and White Sheet Films*.

3. Photographing in Color

We are used to seeing the world in color. When we look at reproductions of our world, color reproductions are preferable. Advertisers long ago learned that color advertisements do a better selling job. Many consumers, happy for over two decades with a black-and-white television set in the living room, have decided that they would rather have a color set. Magazine features of importance generally offer illustrations in color. Color communicates better than black-and-white, and in most instances, color costs more.

When the new photographer first loads his camera with color film, his instinct is to take pictures of the most colorful objects he can find. The color screams! If we accept the color photograph as a device for communication, or for establishing mood, color falls correctly into place as one creative element among several. Even objects that we normally think of in mono-chromatic terms have color that adds to their richness and quality. Subtle colors can be as moving and exciting as blatant ones. Excellent textbooks for color still-life photography are available on every newsstand in the fine magazines. The so-called shelter-books, such as *House and Garden, House Beautiful,* and the top-quality general readership magazines such as *Life* carry the work of the best still-life photographers as advertising for food, tableware, furniture, and other products. One thing to note in studying these advertisements is that color has not been used as a device to replace photographic skill and careful technique. It becomes, in skilled hands, an additional tool to communicate a visual message.

There are basically two types of color film with which you can load your camera: negative film and reversal film. Like black-and-white negatives, color negatives must be reversed in printing after development to produce recognizable colors. Reversal, or transparency, films are processed directly into color transparencies.

COLOR PRINTS

The color print is superior to the slide or transparency for many purposes because it can be seen in normal room light without special equipment. For selling or similar situations, when only a few people are trying to organize or compare a series of images or objects, color prints are easily sorted, resorted, and arranged. Prints can be carried, mailed, or hung with little trouble. They can be used as supplements to actual samples on exhibition, and in a portfolio color prints can do yeoman service! They are highly portable, and if reasonable care is observed in their storage, they are quite permanent. They offer a *total* impression of a subject.

For the photographer, films which produce a color negative hold a number of advantages over the positive, or reversal, color films. Exposure latitude, while not as great as black-and-white, allows for greater error than in slide making. You can expose color negatives from at least one-half stop under correct exposure to one and one-half stops over and still get good prints. If you are not equipped with the proper filter to match a particular film to a light source at the time of exposure, overall color corrections can be made through filtration when the color negative is printed. (This will not help you, though, if you mix light sources of different color temperatures.)

If color accuracy is your aim, as it generally will be, the inclusion of a neutral gray or color test card at the edge of your photograph will help the laboratory making your color prints to filter for true color.

The same flexibility of control that allows the making of highly accurate color prints also gives the advanced worker the opportunity to experiment with color in the printing process to create mood and special effects. You can, for instance, introduce polarizing screens, special filters, or bands of gelatin over your original negative, when printing, to try to achieve a special effect, without altering or destroying your original negative. If they do not work, you can always try something else.

Prints can also be made from positive color slides such as Kodachrome or Ektachrome transparencies. But photographic prints from positives are generally more expensive and less satisfactory. Such prints do not hold details in the shadows as well as prints made from color negatives. Colors lack the brilliance and clarity that can be obtained with negative processes. One can get superb results from dye-transfer prints, which are made from a negative made from a transparency, but their high cost restricts their use to the type of commercial situation in which the cost of a print is a secondary consideration.

Color negatives can also produce excellent transparencies in the original size, or larger or smaller sizes. Because most color-negative films have a built-in mask, transparencies and slides of excellent color quality will result without need for the expensive masking procedures that are required to control excessive contrast buildup when making duplicate slides or enlarged transparencies from original positive transparencies.

Opposite

Top:

A catalog photograph should show the product illustrated in use. In this case, the glass of wine and candles in a simple holder suggest a mood of elegance. The color photograph and the copy indicate all three colors — white, yellow, blue — in which the items are available. Food props further suggest possible uses. The black vignette at the top of the photograph was created to allow the printer to "drop in" copy for the catalog cover. It was achieved by using a 6" lens on a 4" x 5" view camera and then lowering the lens board so that a part of the film was outside the circle of illumination provided by the lens. This also eliminated unwanted room detail. Lighting was by two 500-watt incandescent bulbs (3200° K.) bounced off the room's white ceiling.

Bottom left:

This selling photograph shows transparent boxes in a range of colors and with three types of cover. A variety of box shapes and sizes are shown, and the fact that the boxes will ship or store nested is also illustrated. Simple line drawings or a black-and-white photograph showing other sizes and shapes of plastic boxes could easily be used with this single color picture to illustrate an extensive line of boxes.

For this picture the view camera was adjusted with its back parallel to the front plane of the boxes, and the board was tilted forward to obtain the maximum depth of field. The lighting was provided by a light table illuminated from below by two 500-watt lights under opal glass and a spotlight high and to the right of the subject to illuminate box outlines and detail. Shadows were eliminated by a higher degree of illumination under the light table than in shadows thrown by the spotlight above. A 240 mm. Tele Arton lens was used on a 2¹⁄₄"-square negative, after moving the camera away from the subject to achieve the proper perspective.

Bottom right:

A less clearly explanatory but graphically more exciting photograph of the boxes shown at left was made by photographing the boxes on a piece of white no-seam to accentuate a shadow pattern. Product color and other product features are still shown, but not as descriptively. If one were making a cover for a brochure describing products of this type, such an illustration might command more attention than the preceding photograph. Descriptive drawings and/or photographs in the brochure could then pick up the burden of detailed explanation. The boxes were photographed on a no-seam paper background and illuminated by a single 500-watt spotlight to the right and rear of the subject. (See diagram below.)

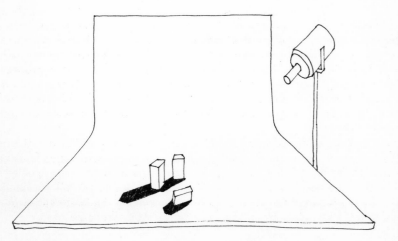

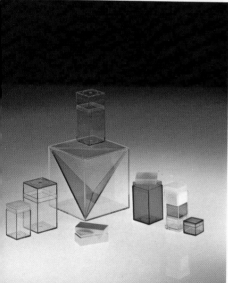

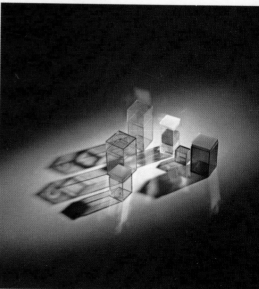

The new color-negative materials are so flexible that even good black-and-white prints can be obtained from color negatives, if they are printed on the special black-and-white papers designed for that purpose, such as Kodak Panalure.

To me, the best slide is one made in the camera on a reversal film designed for slide-making, just as the best black-and-white print is obtainable from a black-and-white negative. But it is nice to know you can use the almost universally obtainable color-negative films to produce good-quality results in other forms than the color print.

Color prints are still, popular as they have become, much more expensive than black-and-white prints of equivalent size. However, the very fact that they show color makes them more effective for sales and presentation use than even high-quality black-and-white prints. In the matter of size, for instance, a post-card-size color print for thirty cents might do a better presentation job than the finest 8″ x 10″ black-and-white. Furthermore, because color defines pattern and areas more clearly than black-and-white, considerations of definition are often less important in delivering a literal message about an object.

As with black-and-white photography, the success of color prints depends on two operations: the skill of the photographer in making the negative, and the expertise of the processor who makes the print. Even when the same material, such as Ektacolor paper, is used, color prints will differ according to the way the material is handled.

There are two types of processing laboratories. One mass-processes prints and film by machine and the other handles each negative separately. Even within these two categories, there are, of course, broad degrees of qualitative difference. From your point of view as a photographer, however, there is one key factor. The custom laboratory can work with subtle degrees of difference in filtration and will test and retest to give you the best possible print from your negative, while the machine processor works with a limited number of standardized procedures. He cannot work and rework your print for thirty cents or even for three dollars. You pay more for custom service because you are buying the time of a skilled technician.

You can get good results from machine laboratories if you plan for it. When making a negative for automatic or standard processing — the kind most photography stores offer — remember that all interpretive or creative manipulation and all controls must be exercised *in the shooting*. Most automatic processors cannot or will not make corrections to any marked degree in printing. At the time of exposure you must put into the negative: correct exposure; color temperature ranges satisfactory to the processor; correct composition within a standard print format; any required or desired corrective filtration. It is a good idea to include a color scale at the edge of any still-life photograph — or at least on one negative in a series — to guide the printer, but most automatic laboratories will not correct to a color scale unless enough prints are involved to make it worth their while.

34

Sunlight is the best light for crisp, clean color. In this photograph, the client wanted to accentuate the shell-like shape of his ashtrays. What better place than a sandy beach? A piece of driftwood supplied a means of making an interesting grouping and provided a nice textural contrast to the slick glass. A slightly overcast sun provided soft shadows, and the light sand acted as a reflector to fill in shadow areas. The camera used was a 9″ x 12″ Linhof, loaded with Ektacolor-S film.

In regard to exposure, a custom laboratory will print for that part of the negative that you tell them is important. In automatic printing, however, exposures are set by the overall density of the negative. There, the important part of your negative and subject must be dominant. If you give a snapshot photofinisher a picture of a small subject on a large background and the exposures on the subject and background differ widely, you are likely to get a correctly exposed background on your print, with the subject badly over- or underexposed.

Fill your film with a composition that will not have to be cropped. Make what is on your negative fit a standard $3^1/_2''$ x $3^1/_2''$, $3^1/_2''$ x $5''$, $5''$ x $7''$, or $8''$ x $10''$ machine print. Crop the actual negative with a tape mask to insure proper proportions, if necessary. Most machine processors expect to print a negative exposed by daylight or by blue flash. Therefore, check the instruction sheet that comes with your film to see what filter you need with your studio lights to produce a negative with the same final color balance as if you had exposed your picture by daylight. For example, Kodacolor-X, its direction sheet tells us, is balanced for daylight; for shooting in daylight no filter is required. But the slip recommends the use of an 80A filter when you expose Kodacolor-X under 3200°K. studio lights. These lights are "warmer" than daylight, and the blue filter restores the light reaching the film to a balance approximating daylight. If you shoot a lot of Kodacolor-X under 3200°K. lights and tell a laboratory willing to use filters in printing to correct the color balance, they can do so. The cheaper machine-processing plants, however, are not likely to take the trouble. A phone call might tell you to what extent a photofinisher will cooperate. If you give him a properly balanced negative to begin with, he can print it as he prints a negative produced in daylight, and the result will be well-balanced color. Note that most such filters reduce the effective speed of color film, but this is not likely to be a serious limitation in still-life work.

COLOR SLIDES AND TRANSPARENCIES

For most amateurs, and, for that matter, most professionals, color photography for the past three decades or so has meant color slides or transparencies. Even with the development of excellent color-negative films and print materials, the slide has retained its popularity for several good reasons. Slides can deliver exceptional color fidelity. The excellent processing services available from the major manufacturers for their own films are, and always have been, kept at a very high level. Many local laboratories which process color positives also do consistently good work. For control and color accuracy, slides are still generally superior to most print processes.

Kodachrome is very nearly grainless, and other transparency films offer excellent grain characteristics — to the point, in fact, where grain can almost be eliminated from the photographer's considerations. Sharpness, insofar as it depends on the film and its processing, can be taken for granted. The superb photographs which fill the *National Geographic Magazine* year after year are usually reproduced from small transparencies, most often 35 mm. Kodachrome slides. While they might not meet the standards of an advertiser looking for superb detail in a full-color, full-page advertisement, they would be considered more than adequate for most purposes.

Slides are most often thought of as 35 mm. slides for projection. However, 35 mm. cameras, even when equipped with trick bellows attachments, do not offer the flexibility of the larger-format cameras with which you can control depth of field and make perspective corrections in the studio. Transparency films do come in larger roll-film sizes and popular cut-film formats.

If your aim is projection, stay with 35 mm. slides, but if you also need perspective correction, you might consider the emulsions available in 120 roll film. This size will produce $2^1/_4''$-square transparencies, which most laboratories will mount for you as a matter of course. Most modern 4″ x 5″ view cameras which offer such perspective control will accept roll-film adapters, and there are a number of relatively inexpensive and portable projectors made to show these larger transparencies. As you would expect, these films, with their 300-percent greater area, produce pretty exciting detail and color when projected and offer quality advantages when used for reproduction in color printing. The larger $2^1/_4''$ x $3^1/_4''$ roll-film negative and cut-film sizes up to 8″ x 10″ have great advantages for direct viewing without projection and offer the critical worker a better medium in which to prepare work for the editor or printer.

When you make a mistake in exposing a transparency, there is no second chance for exposure correction in printing as there is with color-negative film. The processing is generally standard. If you shoot with some emulsion — not Kodachrome! — where "processing by user" is possible, a good custom laboratory can make minor corrections to compensate for exposure errors, but you have to advise them *before* they process what you think the degree of over- or underexposure was. For insurance, many professionals make three "bracketed" exposures of a single subject and setup. Practically speaking, this means that you make one exposure exactly as indicated by a meter reading of the most important part of your subject. A second exposure is then made at one-half stop less than the reading and a third at one-half stop more. Since the range of exposure tolerance of most color reversal films to hold accurate color is only about two stops, many photographers will bracket exposures one stop over and under. Your meter should be sufficiently accurate to permit working within a half-stop range. A lack of latitude in reversal color films also indicates less contrasty lighting than you might wish to use for most photographs made on black-and-white or negative color film. I find that a lighting ratio of not more than three to one from the lightest to the darkest part of the scene will normally produce the most pleasing results for a descriptive commercial photograph. It can be expanded to a four-stop range in some cases, but this would be fairly

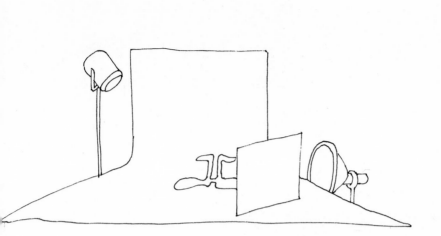

Opposite:

The white plaster figure with polychrome decoration illustrates a typical problem with the photography of opaque, irregularly shaped objects. A spotlight high and to the rear left of the figure defines its shape. A highlight on the man's head separates it from the gray no-seam background. A strong fill-in light to the right of the subject balances the spotlight, and a cardboard reflector to the right of the camera and close to the subject fills in the frontal shadows. Note that the shadow cast before the figures adds to the pattern interest. Since it was impossible to produce a highlight on the head of the female figure, a bit of white chalk rubbed on the figure was used to outline the head before shooting.

Regardless of how good a black-and-white photograph may be, in cases where color is an important part of the design, nothing but a color presentation of the product will deliver full product appeal. Compare these photographs with their black-and-white counterparts on pages 107 and 121. Which makes the product more appealing? Note that the reproductions on page 38 are small. Big, expensive color prints are not always necessary, although they are more dramatic. The lighting used was identical to that employed for the black-and-white photographs. Photographs on Ektachrome, Type B, roll film.

Opposite:
While we tend to think of some objects as having very little color, these almost monochromatic objects invariably are better explained by full color photographs when the budget permits.

Above left:
Even a pressed crystal goblet shows many hues in a color photograph. A bit of "wine" (vegetable color in water) is reflected in the facets of the glass, highlighting them (see diagram on page 116). The goblet was placed on a sheet of clear glass in front of a black card. Two small spotlights, one directly below the goblet and a second to the right of the subject provided illumination (see lighting diagram). A higher-than-subject camera angle was used to illustrate the round top. The camera bed was dropped to lower the image on the film, and the back and board of camera were then swung vertically.

Above right:
The product itself is perhaps shown no better here in color than in a black-and-white picture. However, the use of a bright orange measuring scale adds impact to the design. Color invariably draws more attention to the product.

Below left:
In this primitive African bronze sculpture we have one answer to the argument that everyone knows what color bronze (or stone or whatever) is. Do we? Most people looking at the actual object would not consciously register the variation in metallic hues that show under the bright lights of the studio.

Below right:
A simple black and birch Kokeshi doll could be illustrated adequately in black-and-white, but color tells the whole story. A light gray no-seam background and a three-light setup were employed to impart roundness to the object (see lighting diagram on page 110). A 500-watt spotlight at the same height as the subject provided the main light. The floodlamp to the right of the subject was placed below it to eliminate any second and conflicting shadow. Behind the subject, a small 125-watt spot was placed above the background to add a highlight on the doll's head. This highlight describes the almost polished texture of the head. The three-to-one lighting ratio is strong for color but was needed to show the roundness of the planes. The camera back and board were parallel to the base of the subject in order to avoid distortion.

extreme. Special effects are another story, of course, and if your subject or scene will tolerate loss of detail in part and some shifts of color at the extreme light and dark ranges, you may wish to experiment with harder, more contrasty lighting. However, change your lighting to within the above limits for some of your exposures before you experiment, unless you are prepared to do the whole job over again.

Slides and transparencies can be duplicated, but the results are seldom a substitute for the original. The inexpensive slide duplicating services offered most amateurs are generally less than satisfactory. If duplicates are properly masked by a custom laboratory, they are expensive. The villain is contrast. Each time a slide is duplicated, the duplicate shows more contrast than the original. Consequently, if you know you are going to duplicate a given slide, or for that matter make a positive print from it, keep the contrast buildup in mind and try to make a flat, evenly exposed transparency. Light slides that are slightly overexposed and show a minimum of shadow and contrast tend to print and duplicate best.

USING FILTERS IN COLOR PHOTOGRAPHY

The best kind of filter to use in a studio situation is none at all. If you are using a film balanced for the color temperature of your light source, you need none. There are times, however, when you might not be able to obtain exactly the film you want, or when you might wish to expose under different light sources on the same roll of film. In such cases, conversion filters are a simple and satisfactory answer.

Conversion filters allow you to use daylight film under artificial light, or indoor film in daylight, and still obtain natural and pleasant color rendition. However, there are various types of artificial light, and each type has a different characteristic color, or, as it is expressed in photographic terms, a different color temperature.

Color temperature derives from the fact that a theoretical black body, heated until it glows, will produce a color directly proportional to its temperature. Color temperature is measured in degrees Kelvin (K.). The tungsten filament in a lamp is close enough to the theoretical black body that its temperature can be used as a description of its color. For practical purposes, higher color temperatures tend toward the blue range of the spectrum and contain, proportionately, less red. Thus, daylight has a high color temperature (plus or minus 6500°K.). Studio light sources offer a lower temperature. Thus, when you use a color film balanced for daylight indoors with artificial light (not a good idea unless you have to), you need a bluish filter to correct the color and, when an indoor film, balanced for lower color temperatures, is used in daylight, an orange tone or filter should be employed.

Here are some examples of color temperatures:

daylight: 5500°K.
blue flashbulbs and electronic flash: similar to daylight
zirconium-filled, clear flashbulbs (AG-1, M-3, M-5): 4200°K.
aluminum-filled, clear flashbulbs (M-2, M-5, M-25, etc.): 3800°K.
photoflood lamps: 3400°K. (when new)
standard studio lamps: 3200°K.

Other types of artificial lighting for photographic purposes generally are furnished with information on color temperature or have the color-temperature rating printed right on the bulb. You lose less speed converting a film balanced for use with tungsten lighting to daylight use than you would using daylight film indoors. For this reason, indoor film is your best choice when you might have to mix lighting conditions for different shots on a single roll.

Unfortunately, the most widely distributed roll films are balanced for snapshot purposes rather than professional use, and, if you are equipping a studio with 3200°K. lamps, you may find you must adapt daylight films or 35 mm. indoor films which are balanced for 3400°K. amateur photofloods.

The instructions packed with most color films give color-conversion filter data on the instruction sheet that comes with the film, but for reference, tables are included in an appendix.

It is possible to make studio photographs for years with highly satisfactory results and never use filters other than conversion filters. However, it is well to know that other standard color-control filters exist for especially critical color control.

Compensating filters are used for very critical results in correcting minor variations in the balance of color. For exact results, you might test film — reversal type film especially — by viewing the test results through compensating filters and decide to shoot again through the filter that makes the desired correction. Compensating filters are generally available in yellow, to absorb blue; magenta, to absorb green; cyan, to absorb red; red, to absorb blue and green; green, to absorb blue and red; blue, to absorb red and green. Each color can be obtained in graded densities, which require small exposure increases depending on density, and filters may be used in combination although combinations of more than three should be avoided, since they may affect lens definition. A table is included in an appendix.

Color- balancing filters are similar to conversion filters but are graded in smaller steps to effect smaller changes in color temperature. Using a filter of a bluish cast is equivalent to raising the color temperature of a light source, while the use of a filter with a yellow cast would produce results similar to using a lower color-temperature light source. The blue filters, of course, produce colder results, while the yellow filters give colors a warmer appearance. Such balancing filters are useful, as you become more critical of your results, to induce an element of mood into your photographs.

While filter recommendations, and even filter designations, may vary depending on the manufacturer, I have found that a filter that will produce a given result on a Kodak daylight film will produce similar results when used with a GAF, Agfa, or Perutz film made for daylight shooting. In other words, the shift in color balance caused by a filter will be similar on a film similarly balanced for a given temperature of light source. When departing from the manufacturer's recommendations, a test is a good idea.

RECIPROCITY FACTOR

A film's rated speed may change with unusually long or abnormally short exposure times. Every film has a range of normal exposure times for which it was designed. The speed changes which take place are due to the reciprocity factor of that film. Familiar outdoor conditions seldom lead to much variation in either respect. Studio conditions can force much greater degrees of variation in light level and exposure time. While, mathematically, one unit of light reaching the film for ten seconds would appear to be equal to ten units of light for one second, this is not so photographically. The exposure latitude of black-and-white film is so wide, for all practical purposes, that this shift can be disregarded. However, in color the latitude of exposure is far more limited, especially when you are exposing reversal films, and a slight shift will be immediately visible in the results obtained.

Normally, in shooting transparencies, no object in the scene should require more than two stops greater exposure than the principal subject (midpoint reading on your meter) to record detail, nor should it be more than four times as bright, or require reducing exposure by more than two stops before detail is blocked by overexposure. Considering that a half-stop change in exposure is visible enough to require bracketing of exposures in most color work, you can see that a small change in film speed due to a change in the length of exposure time can become critical. For example, Kodacolor-X roll film exposed in a studio under 3200°K. lights with a Kodak 80A filter would have a rated speed of A.S.A. 20 at all shutter speeds from one to 1/1000 second. If you are forced to expose for ten seconds, however, the data sheet for the film advises you to give your film one stop additional exposure — to double the exposure. Professional color film is packed with sheets giving such information; these sheets should be carefully studied. In the case of most color cut films, each batch is tested and any significant variations are noted for the particular batch on the information sheet.

Color shifts which occur with changes in exposure can be as important as film speed variations. Consider the fact that color film has three emulsion layers, each a different color. These layers may not only change speed during longer or shorter exposures than those for which the film is designed, but, to make matters worse, the speed of each layer may change differently. Obviously, such differences in the speed of the three primary color layers can upset the color balance. For this reason, color compensating filters as well as changes in exposure times are often recommended by the film

44

manufacturer. While such color shifts can usually be corrected in printing with negative films, there is no chance for such correction once a transparency has been processed, except, perhaps, through the messy solution of binding it in a mount with a compensating layer of gelatin filter material.

The best solution is to pick a film designed for your type of shooting and lights and thus eliminate the need for filters. However, if a small aperture is demanded by a shot that requires great depth of field, or if there is inadequate lighting to cover an area that is larger than usual, check the film instruction sheet very carefully to see if you must correct the exposure time or color balance.

COMPENSATION FOR LENS EXTENSION IN CLOSEUP WORK*

Normally photographers work at distances from a subject which do not greatly extend a lens from its shortest position (infinity setting) on the camera. In photographing small objects, however, we often must move the camera closer to the subject in order to fill the negative. To bring the subject into focus, you must then move the lens farther away from the film plane. On a view camera this is accomplished by extending the bellows. Most view cameras provide at least a double-extension bellows — a bellows which will rack out to twice the focal length of a normal lens. On many cameras with removable lenses a similar result can be achieved by the use of a supplementary bellows attachment or extension tubes. The lens is removed from the camera body, the extension device fastened to the camera body in place of the lens, and the lens then mounted on the front of the extension device. Still greater magnification can be achieved by using a shorter-than-normal lens on the camera and extending it.

When you extend your lens, you change its effective speed. An f stop is based on the aperture (the size of the lens opening) divided into the focal length of the lens. The formula could read $f = \frac{\text{focal length}}{\text{lens opening}}$. Thus, to find the speed, or effective f stop, of a six-inch lens with a one-inch opening, the formula would read $f = \frac{6}{1}$, or f/6. Rack out that lens to twelve inches to achieve a 1:1 (actual size) reproduction of the subject, and you see that the new formula is $f = \frac{12}{1}$ and the effective stop is reduced to f/12. Actually, this is not a practical way to calculate increased exposure to compensate for the long bellows extensions, since you cannot measure the size of the diaphragm opening and figure out a mathematical formula each time you refocus. There are many tables and calculators available for this purpose, including an excellent one in the Kodak *Master Photoguide,* which require only that you measure bellows extension. The best way, if you are going to do much closeup work, is to mark your bellows attachment increase factors on your camera bed or standard.

*See mathematical formula for increased exposures due to lens extension in Appendix C.

Compensation for lens extension can generally be ignored, provided that your subject is at a distance from the camera equal to at least eight times the focal length of your lens. If you are working with a two-inch lens, you need not worry about it if you are at least sixteen inches away; with an eight-inch lens, you are safe if you are sixty-four inches away from your subject. However, if you are closer, especially if working with color film, you should compensate for the increased extension of your lens.

One method is to compare the size of the image on the film (through the groundglass) with the size of the subject being photographed. With some practice, image magnification can be reasonably estimated. For example, if you are filling about one-half of a $2^1/_4$"-square negative with an object, you have an on-film image about one inch high. If you know the object you are photographing is five inches high, you have a one-fifth magnification. Use the following table to calculate exposure increase based on image magnification.*

Magnification	Exposure Increase
(when image is smaller than object)	
1/5 (1:5)	1.4X
1/4	1.6X
1/3	1.8X
1/2	2.3X
2/3	2.8X
3/4	3.1X
(image and object same size)	
1/1	4.0X
(when image is larger than object)	
1.5:1	6.3X
2:1	9.0X
3:1	16.0X
4:1	25.0X

*Additional formulae for calculating magnification ratios and exposure adjustments may be found in the appendix.

The easiest way to use your meter to incorporate a bellows extension exposure factor is to divide the speed of the film you are using (A.S.A. rating) by the factor and then reset your meter to the newly calculated film speed. For example, if you are using a film rated at A.S.A. 80 and shooting a 1:1 magnification ratio for which the increase factor is 4, you would divide 80 by 4 and set your meter for a film speed of 20.

COMMON ERRORS IN COLOR PHOTOGRAPHY

There are some general pitfalls which apply to any sort of color photography and which should be reviewed here:

Do not mix color temperatures. You can correct an entire negative in color from daylight to artificial light, or the reverse, but if you have mixed two light sources of different color temperatures on the same negative, there is nothing you can do to restore correct color balance.

Watch out for colored reflecting surfaces. If, for example, you are shooting a string of pearls on a green background, you are probably going to have green pearls. A green background will reflect green light. This can be especially troublesome out-of-doors where a green lawn or tree or a red barn door can raise havoc with subject colors. Our eyes adjust to reflected color. The camera lens and film do not.

Care in the storage of color film before and after exposure is also necessary if you are to avoid loss of speed and changes in color. This is also true of black-and-white film, but as we have seen, speed variations in color work are more apparent. To avoid disappointment try to avoid keeping film at high temperatures or in very humid conditions. If you are working in a warm, wet climate, keep your film in a refrigerator, but take it out in a closed container (the one it is packed in) for several hours before using it. This will prevent moisture from condensing on the film.

Standardize on one good processor. Most manufacturers offer excellent processing services for their products.

Lenses can vary in color rendition. Try to use the same or matched lenses from the same manufacturer.

Very few shutters are absolutely accurate as marked. Test yours at the speed ranges you will use most frequently; if they are off, adjust your exposure accordingly.

If you are going to make a number of photographs for a presentation, book, reproduction in a catalog, or any other situation where a number of pictures will be viewed at the same time, and if you desire consistency of color, try to buy all the film you will need for the series at one time and be sure that it is all marked with the same emulsion-batch number. Even the most rigid manufacturing controls will not eliminate all variation in the material. If time permits, you should test a few sheets or a roll under actual shooting conditions before you expose many pictures.

VIEWING TRANSPARENCIES

To show transparencies to their best advantage, there are several types of viewers available. These include projectors, projection viewers, simple viewers that provide transillumination, and some that provide not only illumination but also magnification. Most popular projectors handle 35 mm. slides; some are available that take, in addition, $2^3/4''$-square slides (from 120 film), and a very limited number of projectors accept lantern slides — $3^1/4'' \times 4''$. Units designed for maximum portability can be purchased, as well as highly automated units with a multitude of features you may or may not need. *Photography Directory and Buying Guide,* an annual publication, lists a number of factors to help in selection. I shall review some of the most basic below:

Shorter lenses produce larger images than longer ones if the projector to screen distance remains the same. Standard for 35 mm. is a four-inch lens, for a $2^3/4''$ slide, at least a five-inch lens. If you are going to be projecting for large groups in an auditorium, much longer lenses will be needed to keep image size down to screen size when the projector is far away from the screen. If you will need various focal lengths, be sure they are available for the projector you select.

Optics come before gadgetry. Select a projector that offers even illumination, corner to corner sharpness, good contrast and color fidelity. Ask for a comparative demonstration when you buy.

Lamps commonly vary from 100 to 1,000 watts. A 100-watt projector limits you to a rather small projected size and requires near-darkness. A 500-watt projector gives you a capable at-home projector that will also perform for fairly large group presentations. Over 150 watts, be sure there is an efficient blower cooling system.

Slide changers are probably the most merchandised features of today's projectors. The simplest type is a single shuttle carrier — you push in one slide and take out the one just projected. It is easy to get confused by this device if you do not establish a system of hand loading, but it is simple and nothing jams or breaks down. Stack-loaders and round and rectangular trays to carry slides and feed them into your machine automatically are very popular. Be sure to purchase a machine that uses a popular or interchangeable tray made by a long-established manufacturer. There are dozens of different kinds of tray-loaders and some machines accept more than one type. With devices fancier than these, you are paying for automation, but have a good time inspecting the modern wonders.

Projection viewers are essentially small projectors with wide-angle lenses that throw an image on a screen that is part of the unit. Rear-illuminated screens vary in size up to almost a foot square. These very portable viewers are probably most useful for sales presentations to one or a few people.

The simplest viewer is a rear-illuminated piece of flashed opal or ground glass, evenly lighted from the rear. For large negatives such large viewing frames or tables are essential. For negatives 2³/₄″ square or smaller there are dozens of plastic devices with and without built-in light sources that cost between one and ten dollars. These viewers are of great help in inspecting and sorting slides. Some viewers are actually racks which permit the viewer to see many slides at one glance, and are most useful in putting together a presentation. One well-designed unit can be purchased for under five dollars. A transilluminated light box used for shooting pictures in the studio can double as a transparency viewer, but you will probably want to change the bulbs for bulbs of a higher color temperature.

If you want to build your own viewing/sorting device, follow these guidelines for most satisfactory results:

If used in a dim room, an illuminator would need a value of 160 candles per square foot (most exposure meters will measure foot candles).

In a daylight situation, values as high as 285 candles per square foot may be required.

Studio lights are not the best choice for viewing as they may lack sufficient blue and green light to produce pleasing colors. Choose whiter lights from 3800°K. to a more ideal 5000°K.

In general, view and judge your transparencies under the conditions most nearly approximating those under which they will be shown to others. Prejudging under other than actual viewing conditions can be misleading.

JUDGING TRANSPARENCIES FOR THE PRINTER

Transparencies in larger sheet-film sizes, 4″ x 5″ and up, are used principally for photomechanical reproduction — the printing of ads, catalogs, and the like. Such transparencies should be viewed for detail especially in highlight and shadow areas. Overly harsh, contrasty lighting is perhaps the most frequent thief of detail at either end of the tonal scale. On viewing a transparency in a dimly lit room, you may be able to see detail that a printer cannot reproduce. He will tend to drop borderline detail in either very dense or very light areas of the transparency. A transparency given slightly less than the exposures indicated as normal by the meter often produces better highlight details in printing. View your transparency, if possible, in a normally lighted room on an illuminator larger than the transparency itself. When you have made a few transparencies, meet with your printer and get his criticism of your work.

SOME POPULAR KODAK COLOR FILMS

Film Name	Type	Color Balance w/o Filters	A.S.A.* Speed	Sizes Available
Kodacolor X	Negative	Daylight	80	35 mm., most roll sizes
Ektacolor Professional Type S**	Negative	Daylight	100	Sheet film, 120 & 620 rolls, 35 mm. "bulk rolls"
Ektacolor Professional Type L***	Negative	3200°K.	64	Sheet film only
Ektachrome	Transparency (Reversal)	Daylight	50	Sheets and 120 rolls
Ektachrome Type B	Transparency (Reversal)	3200°K.	32	Sheet film only
Ektachrome-X	Transparency (Reversal)	Daylight	64	35 mm., several roll-film sizes, 126 cartridges
High Speed Ektachrome	Transparency (Reversal)	Daylight	160	35 mm., 120 rolls, 126 cartridges
High Speed Ektachrome Type B	Transparency (Reversal)	3200°K.	125	35 mm., 120 rolls
Kodachrome II	Transparency (Reversal)	Daylight	25	35 mm. & 828 rolls
Kodachrome II Professional Type A	Transparency (Reversal)	3400°K. (photoflood)	40	35 mm. only
Kodachrome-X	Transparency	Daylight	64	35 mm. & 126 cartridges

*speed shown is approximate and based on manufacturer's normal processing recommendations. Index can change with length of exposure, use of filters and other factors. Study data sheet provided with or for most films by the manufacturer before exposing.

**designed for exposures of 1/10 of a second or shorter.

***designed for exposures from 1/10 of a second to 60 seconds.

4. The Selection of a Camera

In the preceding chapters we have reviewed the uses to which you might put the photographs which you will make. You will have decided whether prints (black-and-white or color) or slides best suit your purposes, and whether the photographs you need should be relatively small, say up to 8″ x 10″, or considerably larger, as in the case of exhibition prints.

While you may eventually want more than one camera, most cameras are much more capable than their users, and a thorough familiarity with one instrument is preferable to trying to use several different cameras occasionally. You should know the capabilities and limitations of the camera you use, and this will come only after putting it to the test on the many tasks you set for it and finding out where it performs well and where it does not.

We now enter the realm of personal preference and opinion. If you discuss the choice of an instrument for yourself with a dozen different competent photographers, you will get a dozen different, and probably enthusiastic, recommendations. But there are basic types of cameras which are generally preferred for given types of work, and their popularity in a given field of photography tends to be well deserved. In the right hands, and with sufficient skill and care, almost any quality camera can do a good job. It is up to you to choose the instrument which fills your particular needs with the smallest accumulation of accessories and the least demanding technical processes. There is no camera I know of that is the "best" camera for all types of work.

Fortunately, in selecting a camera for still-life photography, you do not need to buy the most expensive equipment. The qualities that make a camera most desirable in a store and that single it out for current popularity are not necessarily the features you will need, and most of the characteristics which make new cameras expensive are not particularly useful to the photographer using a camera mounted on a tripod. Some of these features are:

Instant-loading. Does it really make any difference whether it takes five seconds or ninety to load your camera?

Built-in metering systems. You will want to use your light meter for readings close to the subject, and will perhaps take readings at several points in the scene you are photographing. You will not want to detach your camera each time to use its built-in meter. Furthermore, the hand-held meter, because it is larger, is generally more sensitive and more rugged.

High-speed shutters. Your subject is not moving anywhere at high speeds. In still-life photography the subject just sits there. Even if there are moving elements in your photographs — perhaps a moving leaf or something else that will not hold perfectly still, a moderate shutter speed of 1/100 of a second will almost always handle it. You *will* need a shutter with a good range of accurate slow speeds, at least one second to 1/25, and a convenient "bulb" or "time" exposure device to enable you to make exposures of more than one second.

For most amateurs, the demand for highest quality in photographic equipment is usually more a matter of prestige than of real need. Each year many thousands of highly precise single-lens reflex cameras are sold in the United States at prices well over $200. In my opinion, they are purchased mainly by amateurs who will never truly test their precision or full capabilities and who purchase them as status symbols.

A fine camera lens is wasted unless you are going to project the picture you make through fine projection optics in a slide projector or enlarger. Cheap processing can destroy the results of the best job in shooting a picture. If you are prepared to buy quality in a camera, you must be prepared to pay for or strive for quality in other aspects of your photographic work. Initially, money invested in good lights, a good tripod, a good meter, and good processing will pay off with better results than if you spend all your money on an expensive camera and skimp on extras. The most important investment the new photographer can make is film: shoot, observe, correct, and reshoot!

Some of the things to consider in buying a camera are discussed below. These include the viewing system, negative size, and the relative merits of used and new cameras.

THE VIEWING SYSTEM

The viewing system is a most important consideration in shooting still-lifes. You will want to examine closely your composition and layout. You will wish to see whether you have the camera completely in focus or not. You must be able to see clearly how and where your shadows fall, which highlights will be recorded on the negative, where unwanted reflections occur. You want to see the picture you are about to record clearly and in detail. One unwanted intrusion into your picture or one overlooked detail can ruin a picture you have worked a long time to set up. While you can get a pretty accurate idea of what is going to be recorded on the film by putting your head in front of the camera and looking at the scene using one eye as a lens, it is not the same as seeing your subject through the taking lens.

Press-view cameras provide the most direct and uncomplicated viewing system. These are larger cameras ($2^1/_4''$ x $3^1/_4''$ to 8" x 10" film sizes, and even bigger) in which a ground-glass panel is slipped into the camera where the film will later be placed. You open the camera lens, and then see an inverted image (to which you become accustomed quite quickly) exactly as it will record on film. Between each shot, the film holder (of which there are different types for cut film, roll film, or filmpack) must be removed and the viewing back repositioned. In my opinion, being forced to work slowly with this type of equipment is an advantage in studio work. It slows you down, demands patience, and forces you to work carefully. In professional still-life work this is by far the preferred type of viewing system. The big 8" x 10" view camera is the studio workhorse. A 4" x 5" view camera is an excellent choice for an amateur who wants to do studio work.

The single-lens reflex camera is, at the moment, the most popular type of camera for serious general use. Like the view camera, it allows you to look through the taking lens. The film remains in place and enables you to make several exposures quickly. A mirror intercepts the light from the lens and reflects it onto a viewing screen or prism, generally located on top of the camera. When the exposure release is pushed, the mirror snaps up out of the way and, at the moment the shutter opens, the light from the lens falls directly on the film. While more convenient than the press-view types, the added complications of a very precise and rapidly moving mirror and a more complex shutter increase the chances of inaccuracies in viewing and the possibilities of expensive mechanical failures. Such cameras are most popular in 35 mm. models, although some excellent 120 models are available. The useful features of lens interchangeability and camera movements may be lacking in such cameras.

The twin-lens reflex camera offers a compromise in viewing. It has long been my favorite type of camera for general photographic use, and is not a bad choice for some types of still-life work. It has two matched lenses, one above the other. One throws an image on a mirror and screen as in the single-lens cameras. The taking lens, mounted below the viewing lens, is always in position to record an image on the film. This type of camera is mechanically more simple than most single-lens models and is less likely to need adjustment and repair, but it introduces another set of problems.

Most twin-lens reflexes will not focus closer than three feet. This is not close enough to fill your negative if you are photographing very small objects. Secondly, the problem of parallax is introduced with many models: because the lenses are mounted perhaps one and one-half inches apart, you do not see, through the viewing lens, exactly what will be recorded through the taking lens. This is of little importance when you are taking a picture of a subject five feet away, but it becomes important when you are working very close to a subject. Generally, twin-lens reflexes do not allow interchangeability of lenses and you may wish, in close work, to use shorter or longer lenses for convenience or to reduce distortion. One camera, the Mamiyaflex, does allow close focusing through the use of a bellows and also allows you to change lenses, but it approaches a small view camera in size and weight without giving you the advantage of being able to see through the taking lens to check depth of field and exact parallax. Unless you are working primarily with objects that you will shoot from a distance of three feet or more, the twin-lens reflex is a poor third choice for still-life work. Most of these cameras make $2^{1}/_{4}'' \times 2^{1}/_{4}''$ negatives on 120 roll film.

Viewfinder and rangefinder cameras should not be considered for still-life work. These cameras employ an optical viewfinder to show you approximately what the picture will look like. They do little more than frame the scene. The rangefinder can automatically set the lens to be in focus; but rangefinders, in general, do not work closer than three feet without complex and cumbersome accessories.

NEGATIVE SIZE

It is true in photography that the larger the negative, the sharper will be the finished picture. This is important technically, but as a practical matter, in many cases there is no need to go beyond a certain point of technical clarity. Then, too, the statement is true only if all other factors are equal; most often they are not.

Larger negatives are most important in black-and-white work, although for really critical color work — as full-page color advertising — there will also be a marked difference in quality.

Since the 8″ x 10″ print has become almost standard for publicity, advertising, and printing reproduction, and is the preferred size for most photographic presentations of merchandise, anything smaller than an 8″ x 10″ negative needs enlarging. There was a time less than fifty years ago when even an amateur who wanted a good print relied on a very large negative. The popularity of the old 3-A Kodaks, which produced a $3^{1}/_{2}'' \times 5''$ negative, attests to that fact. However, with the great improvement in the quality of photographic lenses and in the quality of film and processing techniques in the past twenty years, it is quite possible to obtain quality enlargements even from 35 mm. negatives.

In spite of these remarkable technical advances in photographic technology, the larger negative is still the better choice. I can remember, in the late 1930s, going to a lecture by traveling representatives of E. Leitz, the manufacturers of the Leica camera. Films then were comparatively slow, and grain was a problem. Nonetheless, the speaker exhibited 16" x 20" prints made from 35 mm. negatives which were far better than anything I could get from my much larger equipment. He had something that I lacked, aside from talent and experience. He had the best possible photographic processing facilities at his disposal. A speck of dust in my darkroom, or yours, on a 35 mm. negative can ruin that negative. Similarly, over- or under-exposure destroys print quality much faster in these miniature negatives than in a 4" x 5" negative. The greater the degree of enlargement, the more obvious are your mistakes.

In taking pictures of products, it is desirable to achieve great texture. Black-and-white photographic images are formed by the grouping of grains of silver bromide. The greater the degree of enlargement, the more apparent the grain structure becomes. As it becomes more visible, the lines and masses which make up a black-and-white print tend to lose their sharpness. This becomes especially apparent in very large photographs for exhibition purposes, but since exhibition prints tend to be viewed from a greater distance, this fuzziness is not so critical as it is in a print to be viewed from close quarters.

Tonality in a print is also, to some extent, a matter of negative size. The broadest range of tones, from a true black to a clean white with clearly defined grays in between, will probably be found in a contact print. Smaller negatives tend to lack the rich, full tonal scale frequently found in large-format work. If extremely skillful processing is employed and great care is exercised in the printing of a small negative, it is sometimes possible to obtain full tonal richness in a miniature camera enlargement, but generally, the better clarity of results from larger negatives is clearly noticeable.

If processing is less than perfect, which it frequently is, or if a dust spot or scratch occurs on a large negative, it is not enlarged to the same degree as on a small one. If retouching is to be employed to improve a photo, a 4" x 5" negative is about as small as even an experienced retoucher would care to work with.

In shooting color, much of what I have outlined above is of less consequence. First, Kodachrome, and to a lesser extent perhaps, other color films, are practically grainless. Furthermore, color tends to define masses and lines much more satisfactorily than shades of gray. Therefore, color pictures seem sharper than black-and-white prints. We are accustomed to seeing the world in color, and we thus look at a color photograph without having to reinterpret the images and add color mentally. When you see a small enlargement from a box camera in black-and-white, you may well notice that clarity is somewhat lacking. If you saw the same snapshot in color, it would better satisfy your need for detail. When you put a 35 mm. color slide in a projector and, for example, fill a forty-inch screen, you are enlarging in the extreme. If you walk up to the screen, you will see that the sharpness is only apparent, but from a distance of over six feet, the color definition supplies the needed definition.

Perhaps for this reason, the convenient and flexible 35 mm. camera, with its tiny negatives, has almost taken over the field of color photography. The photographer who shoots small models and does not want to magnify each imperfect detail relies on a miniature negative to soften detail. Most advertising photographs of top quality are still made from large negatives.

Below are my recommendations on how best to use films of various sizes.

35 mm. film is good for slides, fair for color prints up to 8″ x 10″ in size, more difficult for black-and-white prints, especially those over 8″ x 10″.

120 film yields negatives 2¼″ square, 2¼″ x 3¼″, or sizes between. It is fine for color slides, excellent for color prints to at least 16″ x 20″, and excellent, if carefully handled, for black-and-white to at least 16″ x 20″.

4″ x 5″ cut film and filmpack are the most flexible of all. They are for almost any color reproduction need; black-and-white can be enlarged to almost any print size with careful processing. This is the smallest really practical size for negative retouching, and, in my opinion, the size for serious product photography.

8″ x 10″ cut film is superb for color or black-and-white. It is the professional studio workhorse. The film is expensive, as is the processing equipment.

FILM ADAPTABILITY AND INTERCHANGEABILITY

Most studios that work with still-life photography depend heavily, if not almost entirely, on cut film. For practical purposes, if you want a negative larger than 2¼″ x 3¼″, using modern equipment, you have to use cut film. Of the larger sizes available, 4″ x 5″ and 8″ x 10″ offer the broadest range of film types from which to choose. Perhaps more important, because these two sizes are widely used, they are the most readily available. If you buy equipment requiring an odd size, such as 3¼″ x 4¼″, you are likely to find a local dealer out of stock, or at the very least, with a limited choice of emulsions on hand. European sizes such as 9 x 12 cm., while available, are very difficult to get.

In roll film your choice of size is pretty much restricted to size 120 or 35 mm. cartridges. In black-and-white and color transparency film, a more than adequate emulsion range is available in both sizes. But occasionally I have wanted a greater range of color-negative film for special problems than is available in rolls.

One reason cut film is favored is that you can process one sheet. This is helpful if you are only making a few pictures or if you wish to give different sheets different development treatment. You might want to overexpose and underdevelop one sheet to reduce apparent contrast on one shot, and then on another shot do the reverse. Cut film allows you to do this conveniently. On the roll-film side of the fence, users value the ease of carrying a large quantity, the lower film cost, and the ease of processing at home. You should decide which features will be most valuable to you.

If you want to have the best of film worlds, there are many cameras which will use both cut film and rolls. Such cameras are generally in the press- or view-camera categories; they are basically fitted to accept cut film or filmpack in holders, but will take rolls in adapters as well. The Graflock backs, the Linhof system, Mamiya press cameras, and other universal backs permit such interchangeability with great ease. I find that I will use cut-film holders and sometimes filmpack on a short shooting session, whereas, if I have many shots to make, I may use my $2^{1}/_{4}"$ x $3^{1}/_{4}"$ Linhof with two roll-film holders — one for color and another for black-and-white. I can then make both types of negatives without removing the camera from its tripod or even refocusing. Of course, in a camera accepting cut-film holders, you can interchange film just by loading the individual holders with different films, marking them, and using them as required.

CONSIDER THE USED CAMERA

I distinctly remember the cameras I have purchased new in the past thirty years. It is not difficult, since there were very few of them. Unless money is no object, the used market is the place to look for precision equipment. But to know what to look for and where to look requires a bit more counsel and caution.

If I had to pick a year when the modern camera really came of age in the United States, I think I would choose 1937. The view camera, complete with all necessary swings and tilts, has been around since before then. But by then, a practical 35 mm. single lens reflex, and the Rolleiflex, and sophisticated models of the Leica, the Linhof, and the Speed Graphic were all with us, substantially in their present form. In addition, there were a whole flock of $2^{1}/_{4}"$ x $3^{1}/_{4}"$ filmpack cameras which are still not bad choices for still-life photography. Thus there is available on store shelves a selection of first-rate equipment that goes back more than thirty years.

Here are some things to look for in considering the purchase of a used camera:

View cameras are the best choice for serious work. They are 4" x 5", 5" x 7" (with reducing back to 4" x 5"), or 8" by 10". They should have tilts and swings on both front and back for photographing three-dimensional objects. The lens board should rise and shift to the sides and should be interchangeable. Monorail types are easier to focus than those which run on dual tracks and do not make their movements on the optical axis of the lens, but many of the older cameras are still first-class instruments.

Linhof types (Meridian, Horseman, and certain Mamiya models) are my choice for a universal camera. Press-view cameras are compact, portable, take many kinds of film with adapters, offer lens interchangeability, and yet have most of the basic movements of a view camera. Both $2^1/_4''$ x $3^1/_4''$ and 4" x 5" models are available.

Rolleiflex. Older models may lack flash synchronization; many have uncoated lenses and lack some of the latest (and nice) refinements in the viewing system and latest super-formula lenses. However, even the old ones have all the basic features, including quality, that you need to make great pictures when working three or more feet away from your subject. Most imitations lack parallax correction, so buy the original.

Filmpack cameras, of the '30s. A group of popular and sophisticated cameras flooded the United States market from the early 1930s to about 1940. They came in 6 x 9 and 9 x 12 cm. sizes and were and are gems for any serious worker. They offered a full-size ground-glass viewing screen. They are basically designed to use cut film and/or filmpack. The 9 x 12 cm. film-packs are extinct, and cut film is hard to find in that size. There is no problem getting 6 x 9 cm. (or $2^1/_4''$ x $3^1/_4''$) film or pack. The quality models have a double-extension bellows which permit working very close without accessories. They provide rising and falling fronts and usually a side shift, but lack the swinging and tilting movements of the Linhof or view cameras. On the other hand, they are very light and compact and, when available, the best seldom bring over thirty dollars The best-known cameras of this kind are the Kodak Reccomar, Zeiss Ideal and Maximar, Voightlander Avus, and Ihagee. The good ones were equipped with Compur shutters and fine lenses. Be sure you get enough film holders with the camera — they are no longer readily available.

Speed Graphics are little better or worse than the filmpack cameras described above, but they are American, can be bought in a 4" x 5" size, and will do a good job. One in good shape is likely to rival a view camera in price, however, and the view camera is the better buy for studio work.

Single-lens reflexes tell their age. They are complex mechanisms that tend to go out of adjustment more frequently than any other type of still camera. Do not buy one if it is not clean and is not sold with a guarantee. Beware, in these popular types, of anything that looks like a bargain. I have found that even Kodak and Zeiss may refuse to repair older models. So check before buying to be sure parts are available if you need repairs. There are many quality focal-plane makes including Hasselblad, Exacta, Nikon Alpa, Pentax, Miranda, and Topcon. In addition, Kodak, Voightlander, Zeiss, and others made single-lens reflexes with leaf shutters. They should certainly be adequate to most table-top chores, but even the bellows models like the Rolleiflex 66 lack the flexibility of a view camera.

Other points to check in buying a used camera include the following:

Shutter. Leaf types can cost from under ten dollars for a simple cleaning to over twenty dollars if they need repairs. Try them on the slow speeds (one to 1/10 second). Compare them with a new shutter in the shop. You will be able to tell if they are badly off in their timing. Focal-plane shutters are even more expensive to clean and repair; twenty dollars would be a low minimum charge. My advice is do not buy the camera that needs adjustment of its focal-plane shutter.

Lenses. Picture-taking is the real proof of the lens. Even a small chip or scratch may not matter when you try it, but, in general, avoid lenses where the mount has obviously been dropped, dented, or abused. If a lens is mounted in a focusing device that is either difficult to move or too easy in its movement, stay away from it. If cement between elements has begun to turn milky at the edges of a lens as you look through it, or has begun to craze, do not buy the lens.

Bellows. On a larger press or view camera forty dollars would not be unusually high to replace a bellows with pinholes in it or one that was so worn it sagged into the picture area. In a bright room, extend the bellows fully and look at all angles inside. Better yet, try a light bulb inside the bellows in a darkened room. Bellows can be replaced, of course, if the price of the camera is right.

Mirrors. In reflex cameras, look through the lens at the mirror to see if mirror is clouded, scratched, or deteriorating. Ten dollars will fix most of them.

Mechanical features. If an adjustment works hard, or a movement of parts is sticky, be wary. Precision equipment should work smoothly and easily.

The best guarantee of a good buy in a used camera is a dealer you trust, preferably one in your own city. Most businessmen are honest, but get a written guarantee allowing you to return the equipment for refund if you are not satisfied after a week or two.

5. The View Camera

After all is said and done, if you are going to be seriously involved in product photography, there is really just one camera — the flexible or view camera. It is the workhorse of the professional product photographer because of its unique capacity to control perspective. In addition, a high degree of control of the zone of sharp focus is possible with this adjustable camera. Furthermore, the longer-focal-length lenses normally used with a view camera permit longer camera-to-subject working distances, although similar results may be obtained with a longer-than-normal lens mounted on any camera accepting interchangeable lenses.

The problem of controlling perspective and making objects appear natural arises because objects, or parts of objects, closer to the camera photograph larger than those farther away. The tilting or tapering effect which appears when shooting a tall building from below is a familiar case in point. The photographer is closer to the bottom of the building. While the eye adjusts to this condition, the camera cannot unless it can be adjusted mechanically. When you work close to a subject, other distortions occur. Round objects take on an oval shape, and protruding parts near the camera (such as noses or knees) appear disproportionately large. In an attempt to fill a negative, the temptation is to move in close with a short lens. With a longer lens, the camera can be farther from the subject and the effects of foreshortening will be reduced.

Perspective control is not only used to correct distortions; it may also be used to induce distortion for dramatic emphasis. By accentuating angles, increasing the size of one part of an object as opposed to another, you can call attention to a particular feature of an object. Thus, camera flexibility to control perspective can be a creative tool as well as a corrective device.

The view camera looks complicated. In fact, because you can watch the effect of every adjustment on the ground glass, it is perhaps less complicated than figuring out the effects of changes using a camera on which such changes cannot be observed. There are several types of flexible camera. The true view camera offers the following features:

A long bellows draw. This is needed to obtain large images of small objects by extending the lens for close focusing. A long bellows (at least twice the length of a normal lens, or approximately equal to the diagonal measurement of the negative) also enables the photographer to use longer-than-normal lenses.

A back that will swing in both a horizontal and vertical plane. View cameras, especially the new types that swing on the optical axis of the lens rather than from the baseboard or base rail mountings, offer an almost unlimited range of adjustment.

A tilting lens board. Ideally, a lens board that tilts on both a horizontal and a vertical axis is desirable, although one that tilts on a horizontal axis only will generally handle most depth of field problems encountered in still-life work very satisfactorily.

A rising and falling front or a front that moves horizontally (or, on the modern view camera, both). This allows you to correct the lens-to-film relationship as other adjustments are used.

The revolving back. This is a nice feature, since it allows you to tilt the negative without tilting the entire camera; it is hardly vital.

Press-view cameras approximate the adjustments of the true view camera but have more limited degrees of adjustment. Their prime virtue is that they are good hand cameras as well as studio cameras. If you plan to do much of your work outside or at locations remote from your studio, they are well worth considering. A good press-view camera, like the Linhof Technica, is in my opinion the closest thing to a universal camera.

Now let us see how the flexibility and adjustments of the view camera actually work. You will find both the theory and practice of using them easy to master.

CAMERA ADJUSTMENTS

Swing Backs

If the photographic image is to be a correct, reduced, two-dimensional reproduction of the subject, *the film plane must be parallel to the plane of the subject.* This is why the "tilt" or "swing" back on a view camera is so vital.

The primary function of a camera's back movements is to control line relationships. For example, let us assume you are shooting down at a subject placed on a table, a very common situation in still-life work. If you point the whole camera down, and the object on the table you are photographing is standing vertically on the table, your film plane will not be parallel to the object and distortion will result. If you can, on the other hand, point the camera down and then adjust the back to a vertical position, you will cover the object but restore the parallel relationship and a correct perspective of the object. This adjustment is perhaps the most important one in product work.

A horizontal, or "swing," back adjustment can similarly keep parallel relationships. Let us assume you are photographing a cabinet. You want to show the front of the cabinet as a rectangle, but you also wish to show something of the side and top. You must move above and to the side of the subject to make the photograph. If it were not possible to adjust the back, the front of the cabinet would lose its rectangular shape. If you can tilt the camera to cover the subject and then swing the back parallel or nearly parallel to the cabinet front, the problem will be solved. With large subjects, where space is cramped and you must use a short or wide-angle lens, the distortion is even more apparent.

It is a common problem to want to photograph a rectangle as a rectangle but to be unable to place the camera in the center of the subject you are photographing so that the camera axis will be at right angles to the subject. A mural located where a staircase or perhaps a large piece of furniture prevents you from shooting from the center is one example. A store window, where unwanted reflections can be reduced or eliminated by shifting the camera position off center is another. The camera must then be moved toward the side of the object, and the camera back swung parallel to the subject. The rectangle will then photograph as a rectangle.

You can also control depth of field with the swing back, although this is not its primary function; you sacrifice control of line relationships when you swing the back to control focus. Whenever possible, control of focus should be accomplished by swinging or tilting the lens board. There will be times, however, when line distortion is less important than depth of focus. If, in such a case, you find yourself with a camera with a fixed board, or you find the swing of the lens board inadequate to get the depth you want, the back should be swung *in the direction opposite to the plane of the object being photographed.* (See diagram opposite below.) Let us assume you are photographing a table with several objects on it. Raise the camera to cover the table. Then, focus to obtain a sharp image in the center of your ground glass. To bring the objects on the front of the table, which appear at the *top* of the ground glass, into sharp focus, you would have to move the lens farther from the film; but when you tilt the top of the back out, away from the camera (and the lens), you are increasing the lens-to-subject distance for that part of the photograph and bringing those objects into better

62

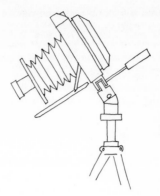

This photograph was made by a camera with all positions "zeroed," as though it were an inflexible camera. Note that the top part of the block, which is closest to the camera, appears larger, and the block seems to taper. In addition, note that sharp focus is not obtained at the bottom of the block in spite of the use of the minimum aperture available (f/45 with a 105 mm. lens).

By swinging the camera back vertically to make it parallel with the principal plane of the subject, the rectangular shape of the block is restored. By further adjusting the lens board, sharp focus is achieved over the entire block surface. The coin was added for scale.

To illustrate fully the block using view-camera adjustments, the block was photographed at an angle. This would normally destroy the rectangularity of the block while still showing the sides and top of the object fully. Here, both rectangularity and sharp focus were retained by swinging the lens board on its vertical axis.

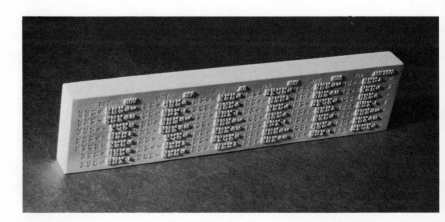

focus, without disturbing the rest of the picture. Now refocus, if necessary. If the objects in the front third of the subject are in focus, stopping down the lens will generally bring the rest of the subject into sharp focus. As always, your critical view of the image on the ground glass will tell you what is happening.

You will find that very noticeable perspective distortion can result from the displacement of the back to gain depth of field. Foreground objects increase disproportionately in size, and shapes change. A spherical shape can become an elipse when back adjustments are used. In enlarging, you

64

The diagram below shows the lighting arrangement. A single spotlight brought slightly forward of the block picked up the texture. Note that where a very dark background was used in the horizontal shots, little light was reflected back into the block to flatten the lighting on the lower part of the block through fill-in light. In the vertical block pictures, fill-in light reduced the effect of the cross lighting.

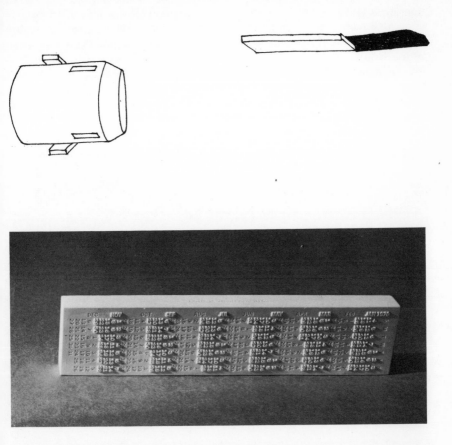

can correct for this distortion, often rather successfully; but this is obviously of no help in a color transparency or color printing if you are not doing your own work. The correction is made by placing the enlarger lens at approximately the same distance from the negative that the camera lens was from the film when the picture was made. (A shorter lens must be used on the enlarger than was used on the camera to accomplish this.) Then tilt the easel holding the paper (or tilt the enlarger head, if possible) to about the same angle as the camera back during the photographing. Actually, tilt the easel until the objects appear in correct proportion.

65

Tilting the Lens Board

The longer lenses normally used on a view camera have a more limited depth of field than those used on hand-held cameras. However, when you can tilt the lens, this problem can be overcome by shifting the plane of focus. Far greater depth of field can be attained by moving the lens board than by stopping down a lens. The best placement of the area of sharpness is obtained when the Scheimpflug rule is observed. This unpronounceable dictum can be seen very simply in the figure, which illustrates that the planes of the lens board, swinging back, and subject, when extended, should all meet in a point.

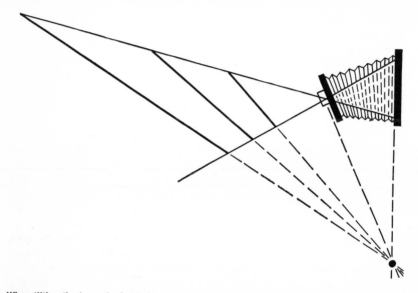

When tilting the lens, the best placement of the area of sharpness is obtained when the plane of the film, the lens plane, and the plane through the subject meet at a common point. Tilting the lens, rather than the camera back, will help to avoid distorting the line relationships of the subject. The principle illustrated by the above diagram is often referred to as the Scheimpflug Rule.

Obtaining a sharp zone of focus to cover your principal subject through moving the lens board allows you to work at full or near full aperture, making maximum use of lens speed. The longer lenses normally used on view cameras are formulated to deliver good sharpness at or near their full openings (with the exception of lenses specifically designed for portrait work and certain wide-angle lenses). While shortening of exposure may not be very important in black-and-white work, color shifts can occur with color films

66

when exposures are extended beyond a recommended limit. Obtaining depth of field without stopping your lens way down can help you to keep exposures within recommended limits.

You will most often use the tilting lens board on a horizontal axis, but there are times when you may want to tilt it on a vertical axis, and many cameras omit this movement. When you are working without a vertical axis adjustment, you can turn the entire camera on its side and achieve the same result using the horizontal-axis adjustment vertically. When your board will not tilt, there is still another trick which involves moving the entire camera to position the lens. Move the lens standard laterally (or, with the camera on its side, raise the board vertically). Aim the camera so that the subject is then centered in the ground glass. Then move the swing back so that it is at right angles to the camera-subject axis.

It is desirable to have a camera which affords both front and back movements. However, any camera which allows you to change the plane of the lens board in relation to the plane of the back will perform in some measure as described above. As you adjust it, simply visualize the lens board and the back as though they could move independently of each other and drop the bed, or use your other available movements to approximate the lens-film position you would achieve with full movements.

The Rising-Falling-Sliding Front

Many fairly simple and primitive cameras have a rising-falling-sliding lens front, a useful feature. The old Speed Graphics and most of the old filmpack cameras built in this luxury of control. Its prime purpose in taking snapshots was to eliminate unwanted foreground, to get in the top of a building, or other tall object, while keeping the camera level, or the film plane parallel to the plane of the subject. In still-life work, in its upright position, this is seldom of use except as a supplementary movement. However, if this is the only movement your camera has, it can be quite useful. Mount the camera using its side tripod socket and then rotate the tripod head 90° so that the camera is upside down and the rising board becomes a drop board.

The lateral adjustments of the lens board can be similarly used in shooting the rectangular subject described above from an off-center position. In brief, the rising and shifting lens board allows a displacement of the lens-film relationship off the optical axis of the lens so that parts of the subject may be included or excluded without disturbing the parallel relationship of film, lens board, and subject.

The Revolving Back

The revolving back has as its principal function slight corrections of image alignment. If a subject is slightly tilted as you view it, you can rotate the back slightly rather than moving the whole camera. However, rotating the whole camera is no great chore. If you have available to you a view camera with all the proper swings and tilts, do not let the absence of a rotating back put you off. It is convenient, but it will not solve photographic problems for you that cannot be solved with only slightly more trouble by simply tilting the whole camera.

PROCEDURE IN ADJUSTING THE VIEW CAMERA

None of the aforementioned rules can become truly meaningful until you have actually worked with a view camera, so I suggest the following sequence in preparing to make a photograph with a view camera: (1) Compose the subject in the ground glass with all camera parts in their normal positions. (2) Swing or tilt the camera back to make it parallel to the principal plane of the subject or to make it *look right*. Learn to check line relationships and perspective distortion when doing so. (3) Swing or tilt the lens board until the sharpest overall focus is achieved. (Remember the Scheimpflug rule to make it easier.) (4) Refocus your camera since the adjustments may have thrown out the exact lens-to-subject distance. (5) Stop down your lens, while watching the ground glass, until the desired degree of sharpness is achieved.

The above will give you a method for tackling any subject, but keep your eye on the focusing screen while you perform each adjustment. Photography ends up in the eye; it should start there. No rules can substitute for the critical eye.

Lens Coverage on the View Camera

Note that when a view camera is used in any position other than that where the negative is placed with its center on the lens-to-film axis, you are using the edges of the image produced by the lens. Unless your lens produces a sufficiently large image, you may "run out of image" as you tend to throw the film, lens, and subject out of a direct line. Having enough image in which to position your film depends on the covering power of a lens. Two factors affect the size of the image that a lens will produce: focal length and angle of view.

Although many of the characteristics of lenses are covered in Chapter 6, these two factors affecting the choice of optics must be reviewed here.

Focal length. You will recall that a normal lens has a focal length approximately equal to the diagonal of the negative it is to cover. Thus, the diagonal of a 4″ x 5″ negative would indicate a lens of approximately $6^3/_8″$ focal length. However, using swings and tilts, you will quickly run out of the image produced by a normal lens. When you throw your adjustments out of their "zeroed" position, a normal lens will not suffice. Thus, if you are going to use the controls built into your view camera, your normal lens should probably be what would be normal for the next larger size, in this case a normal lens for a 5″ x 7″ camera. To make full use of a 4″ x 5″ view camera, especially if you are working with relatively small objects, an 8½″ lens would probably be your first choice. Such a lens will allow you to work farther away from your subject because it will produce a larger image than your normal lens and will afford you a better perspective.

Angle of view is the second consideration. Remember that a 6″ telephoto, 6″ normal, or a 6″ wide-angle lens will produce exactly the same size image of a given subject at a given distance. The angle of view does not depend on focal length, but is quite independent of it. The *angular* covering power depends on the design of a lens, not its length.

Focal length does affect covering power, however. We noted above that a 6⅜″ lens will provide sharp coverage of a 4″ x 5″ negative with a 6⅜″ diagonal measurement, while a 8½″ lens will cover a 5″ x 7″ negative with a diagonal of 8½″. Actually, what we are saying is that a normal lens will produce a *circular* image the diameter of which is approximately equal to its focal length. We think in terms of rectangular images because our negative materials are cut in rectangles, and we can thus use only a rectangular portion of the circular image. Given two lenses of different focal lengths but with the same *angular coverage,* both will record the same amount of the scene from a given camera distance. Thus, when using a longer-than normal lens, your negative will not take in the entire scene unless you move the camera a greater distance from the subject. However, if you are not using the entire scene projected by the lens — and you seldom will in still-life work — but only the part of the scene in which your principal subject is placed, the larger circle of sharp illumination produced by a longer lens will allow you, among other things, to fill your negative with the principal subject and still have a spare illuminated area in which you can work for best composition by shifting the negative area within the larger illuminated circle.

Such a longer-than-normal lens will also eliminate wide-angle distortion. Wide-angle distortion results from the fact that when you shoot a three-dimensional object and reduce it to a two-dimensional photograph, objects at the edge of the field appear wider than those at the center of the field. Where only the center of the field is used, a longer-than-normal lens will tend to eliminate this. The phenomenon does not occur when recording a two-dimensional image, such as a painting, and wide-field lenses, which are shorter than normal, may be used conveniently to cover large two-dimensional objects in a limited space without perspective distortion. Wide-angle distortion cannot be corrected by camera swings.

One way of obtaining a larger-than-normal image within which you can use camera swings and tilts is to use a longer-than-normal lens with a normal angle of view, let us say 55° wide open. (Most lenses increase their angle of view when used at smaller lens stops, and a 55° coverage could usefully increase to about 62° or 63° stopped down.) Obviously, if you use a lens of the same focal length with a greater angle of view, it will provide a larger illuminated circular image of the scene before the camera in which to position the film, in other words, even greater covering power. For this reason, wide-field lenses, such as the excellent Schneider Symmar, which offer a field of view of about 70° of angular coverage, are highly desirable as lenses when the swings and tilts of a view camera are used.

Wide-angle lenses, such as the Schneider Angulons and Kodak Wide Field Ektars, offer a field of view of 85° to 100° which, when used in a focal length equal to the normal focal length of a camera lens, far exceed the demands of photography requiring even the most extreme use of view camera movements. If your subject matter requires the recording of architectural interiors, a wide-angle lens is almost indispensable, but if you are primarily concerned with in-studio, table-top photography, the bugaboo of wide-angle distortion will limit its utility.

One situation in which a highly corrected wide-angle lens would be useful for the type of work discussed herein is in recording two-dimensional subjects where working space is limited. As noted above, wide-angle distortion only occurs in photographing three-dimensional objects. The basic function of the wide-angle lens is to include more of a scene on a negative of given size, at a given camera distance, than a normal lens.

The size of your studio will have a direct bearing on the length of lenses you can use. While every lighting problem is different, and the varying placement of lights, subject matter, and camera will demand different working distances for each photograph, for a 4″ x 5″ negative the following general rule may serve as a useful guide:

Subject Size	Lens Focal Length	Working Space
3′ x 4¹/₂′	8¹/₂ - 10″ (Long-focus lens)	15′
8′ max. dimension	6″ (Normal lens)	16′
10′ max. dimension	90 - 100 mm. (Wide-angle lens)	18′

Obviously, the cheapest and easiest way to get adequate coverage with minimum distortion is to have a large enough studio space and use a longer-than-normal lens.

ROLL FILM ON THE VIEW CAMERA

Most modern view cameras will accept roll-film holders. These offer the great convenience and economy of roll-film cameras and still allow full use of view-camera adjustments. Graflex makes holders for cameras with Graflock backs, Linhof offers a broad range for their own instruments, and Calumet Manufacturing Company makes a versatile roll holder that will slip into any camera accepting a standard 4″ x 5″ film holder. Other sheet film cameras often have special roll-film backs. The maximum negative size generally obtainable with roll holders is $2^{1}/_{4}$″ x $3^{1}/_{4}$″ on 120 roll film.

The popularity of the $2^{1}/_{4}$″ x $2^{3}/_{4}$″ format, which is directly proportional to a 4″ x 5″ or 8″ x 10″ negative or enlarging paper, is growing, and, if you want color slides for projection, Graflex, Linhof, and others make holders that will give you standard $2^{1}/_{4}$″ x $2^{1}/_{4}$″ negatives.

When you put a roll holder on your view camera, you are effectively reducing the size of the camera by limiting it to a smaller negative. However, if you have adequate working space, you can simply move your camera farther from the subject to include more of the scene on the smaller negative. If space is not adequate, you will probably want to buy a shorter lens and have it mounted on a lens board for use with your roll-film back. If you own a wide-angle lens to cover a 4″ x 5″ format, say a 90 mm., this will give you an image on roll film similar to that which a normal 6″ lens will give you on a 4″ x 5″ negative.

All of the above considerations of the flexible camera will only be fully understood when you begin to work with an instrument of this type. Remember that a view camera with all adjustments zeroed becomes a straight camera which can be used just like any inflexible instrument. The additional adjustments, which you will quickly master, offer you a capacity for controlling your image not offered in any rigid camera. Once you have worked with a camera that offers image control through camera movements, you will not be satisfied with making still-life photographs with a less adaptable camera.

6. Lenses—
The Heart of the Camera

A good photographic instrument is a lot more than a lens, but a light-tight box with film at one end and a lens at the other is the starting point for all cameras. The most primitive machines were operated without even a shutter, simply by covering and uncovering the lens. In choosing a camera, a good lens is of prime importance.

What should a photographer planning to take up still-life work look for in a lens and what can he do without? First, the lens must be sharp. It must have good resolving power, the capacity to reproduce detail. Furthermore, a good lens of the proper length will reproduce a high degree of detail right to the edges of the negative, thus permitting the use of the entire negative.

A lens should be color corrected. Most people believe this means a lens will give true color results. Actually, it means that a lens is corrected to focus all colors in the same plane. Most fine lenses, even older ones, do this to a satisfactory degree.

For still-life photography a lens must work sharply close to the subject. Most general-purpose lenses work very well as close as two or three feet and superbly at a distance of five feet or more. Beware the frequently advertised "specials" in photography magazines — the longer lenses that cover big negatives. These sound very much like other lenses, but were computed to be used for aerial photography or long-distance sports coverage. When very close work is required, as in shooting small pieces of jewelry, the lens chosen should be one computed to deliver maximum quality at close working distances. Symmetrical lenses such as Symmar and Caltar S handle both close range work and normal distances well.

Fortunately, for still-life work you do not need those features which most often make lenses expensive. The biggest cost factor in a lens is probably speed. A slow lens of top quality will cost far less than a fast one. In still-life photography speed makes little difference. To get all the desired characteristics into a high-speed miniature camera lens may take a complex formula consisting of as many as six or more optical elements. More elements mean more money. A slower lens of four elements, or sometimes only three, will do a comparable job when speed is not a factor. Zoom lenses often found on today's 35 mm. cameras are of no great advantage in still-life work. In a studio you can always move the camera closer or farther from the subject.

Lens coating applied to reduce internal reflection can generally be recognized by the bluish cast it gives to the glass. It is nice, but not too important in still-life work, where internal flare and diffraction can be reduced by proper lighting and the use of a lens shade. By viewing the subject on ground glass, you can spot any serious flare. Most lenses made prior to World War II were uncoated, and many of superior quality are less expensive because they lack this modern touch.

The famous names of Kodak, Zeiss, Schneider, etc., do not necessarily guarantee top lens quality. All of these companies produced lenses for the economy-minded amateur as well as for professional needs. In used lenses, especially, the good and the bad may be mixed together. An f/2.0 lens that was a standard for Leica in the 1930s, a phenomenon of high speed quality for its time, is available today for fifteen dollars, while its contemporary counterpart, which looks almost the same, will command seventy-five dollars secondhand. The difference is in performance. Comparative prices of used lenses of similar speed are a pretty good guide to quality.

A list of good lenses for product photography which might be found on older cameras would certainly include: *Goerz* — Dagor, Artar; *Kodak* — Ektar, Commercial Ektar; *Rodenstock* — Apo-Ronar (very close work); *Schneider* — Symmar, Xenar; *Voightlander* — Skopar, Apo Lanthar, Heliar; *Wollensak* — Raptar; *Zeiss* — Tessar.

The above are among the most popular and, consequently, the most available brands. There are many others. Ask for a reasonable trial period for any used lens you buy and test it, not on charts, but under the conditions in which you will actually use it. Most experienced photographic dealers will give you good advice in the choice of quality optics.

DEPTH OF FIELD

A lens fitted with an iris diaphragm that will stop down sufficiently can be most valuable to a still-life photographer. While a lens with a large maximum aperture admits more light when wide open and will make viewing easier, this can be offset to a substantial degree by putting a focusing cloth over the viewing screen and your head to cut out extraneous light. Take a few extra seconds for your eyes to become adapted to the dark. Also, a lens of a given focal length with a larger aperture will have less depth of field when wide open, which allows less chance of error in focusing.

Depth of field is the distance from the part of the subject closest to the camera to the part of the subject farthest from the camera that will be in sharp focus. A greater zone of sharp focus will be achieved when a lens is stopped down (used at smaller apertures). For example, let us suppose you are using a 6″ (150 mm.) lens on your camera. Set at a wide-open aperture of f/3.5 and focused at 5′, only those parts of the subject from 4′10″ to 5′2″ would be in focus, thus throwing the background out of focus. This lack of depth of field is highly desirable if you want to throw background out of focus, but not if you need a zone of sharp focus of 2′. If you stopped down to f/16, sometimes the slowest speed on the lens, you would have a zone of sharp focus from 4′3″ to 6′ — good, but not enough to cover the problem. If you had a diaphragm on your lens that could be closed down to f/45 at the 5′ setting, everything would be in focus from 3′6″ to 9′3″ and you would have a sharp zone of almost 6′!

Besides the aperture of a lens, another factor affects the depth of field. Shorter lenses, set at a given aperture, will have much greater depth of field than longer lenses. For example, let us compare three lenses of different focal lengths, all set at an aperture of f/11 and a distance of 5′:

Lens	Depth of Field
2″ (50 mm.) Somar (Zeiss)	3′10″ to 7′2″
6″ (150 mm.) Tessar (Zeiss)	4′6″ to 5′9″
12″ Commercial Ektar (Kodak)	4′10″ to 5′2″

This extreme depth of field is one of the factors that has made the 35 mm. camera with a standard 50 mm. lens, or even the shorter wide-angle 35 mm. lens, such a popular instrument for candid shots. In still-life work, however, you can take the time to focus carefully and use focus creatively. In our examination of the view camera (Chapter 5), we have seen that by moving the lens board, an even greater area of sharp focus can be achieved.

Very few lenses are at their sharpest when wide open. Very fast lenses may have to be stopped down three or four stops to do their best, and even most moderately fast lenses, like an f/4.5, will produce their sharpest image when stopped down two or three stops. A test of your lens is necessary in order to determine its sharpest openings. Two traditional subjects for such tests are a sunlit wall with rough mortar or a page of a newspaper spread out. Shoot such a subject, then check your negative for sharpness, paying careful attention to the edges. If you are not test minded, just make note of the aperture at which you are working with a new lens and view your final results critically.

Stopping way down does not continue to improve sharpness, although depth of field continues to increase. An effect called diffraction tends to reduce sharpness after a certain point. Think of using a garden hose. After a certain point, closing down a nozzle or reducing the opening with your thumb makes the water spread out into a spray. The same thing happens to light passing through a lens at very small apertures. On a 2″ lens, this might be noticeable at f/16 or f/22, while an aperture of f/32 or f/45 might work very well on a good 14″ lens mounted on a studio camera. You must consider this factor when you are tempted to stop down your lenses all the way. When working with first-class optics and enlarging only moderately, such factors tend to be technical facts more than practical problems.

As a practical matter, my recommendation is to buy lenses with at least the following maximum and minimum apertures:

	Maximum Aperture At Least	Minimum Aperture At Least
2″ to 3″ lenses	f/3.5	f/22
4″ to 6″ lenses viewed directly on a ground glass with an Ektalite field lens	f/5.6	f/32
Longer lenses	f/.8	f/45

Generally, lenses not offering at least these maximum apertures are likely to be quite old, computed for a special purpose, or of poor quality for commercial use.

IMAGE SIZE VS. FOCAL LENGTH

When negative size was discussed above, the assumption was made that the full negative area would be used. We then considered the negative as limiting the maximum size of the image recorded. Another factor which determines the size of the image is the focal length of the lens being used. Let us assume you are photographing a vase 11″ high. A 105 mm. lens used at about 4′ will produce an image of the vase on the film approximately 1″ high. A 240 mm. lens used at the same distance produces an image almost 2½″ high. *With the distance fixed, the image size will vary directly with the focal length of the lens.* If a 2″ lens produces an image ½″ high, a 6″ lens at the same distance will produce an image of the same object 1½″ high. A lens three times as long will produce an image three times as large. Note that this has nothing to do with the size of the film being used, unless, of course, the image produced is larger than the film.

75

To obtain maximum quality, it is a big *image* you want, not a big negative alone. You should have a lens long enough to fill your negative at a comfortable working distance from your subject. Note that all 6″ lenses will produce the same size image. The fact that it may be a 6″ telephoto or wide-angle makes no difference. A wide-angle lens of six inches might have a very wide angle of view so that it could be used to cover an 8″ x 10″ film. A standard 6″ lens covers a 4″ x 5″ negative well. However, it is quite possible that a 6″ telephoto design lens made for a 35 mm. camera would cover only the field of 1″ x 1¹/₂″ for which it was designed. The angle of view or ability to cover a larger or smaller negative is an entirely different consideration from the relationship focal length to image size. "Wide-angle" and "telephoto" are terms referring to angle of view of a lens. This consideration is particularly important when using a flexible or view camera, and has been discussed in that section.

The answer to the focal length-image size relationship might seem to be: just move in closer with a shorter lens and the image will get bigger. True, but distortion is likely to become quite pronounced when you do so.

Foreshortening is a very common type of distortion which occurs when the camera is too close to the subject. This can be corrected by moving the camera farther from the subject, but while the distortion is reduced, so is the image size. One answer to this problem is a longer lens. Since you will probably be photographing objects and groups of objects of various sizes and at various distances, you may well need a few lenses of various focal lengths.

Another type of distortion is often blamed on wide-angle lenses. Actually, it has nothing to do with the wide-angle design of the lens, but results from the fact that three-dimensional objects toward the edge of a picture appear wider than objects of the same size at the center. The wider the field of view that is fully exploited to fill a negative, the more pronounced this effect of distortion will become. Without going into further technical detail, a longer lens, producing a desired size of image from a greater distance, will produce less distortion of this type.

You may, at times, wish to use distortion for interest or dramatic effect, but generally, if you are attempting to reproduce accurately a given product, only a limited amount of distortion will be acceptable.

Working distances are critical for other reasons. You want to have room enough to move your lights and vary their intensities by adjusting light-to-subject distance. You have more freedom in the arrangement of your object when camera-to-subject distance is not restrictively close. Therefore, a fair general rule for photographing three-dimensional objects of a scale generally thought of as in-studio subjects of table-top scale would be to equip your camera with a longer than normal lens. I have found the following focal lengths to be generally good for my own type of still-life work with three-dimensional objects:

Camera Size	Normal Lens	Useful Longer Lenses
35 mm.	50 mm. (2")	90 to 105 mm.
2¹/₄" x 2¹/₄"	80 mm.	150 mm.
2¹/₄" x 3¹/₄" (view)	105 mm.	150 mm. and 240 mm.
4" x 5" (view)	150 mm. (6")	210 mm. and 360 mm.

One type of professional lens which offers a normal lens plus a long-focus lens in a single unit is the convertible optic. These have been made over the years under many names, but in design they are all basically symmetrical lenses. This means that the front group of two or three elements is almost identical to the rear group. The most common types offer an increase of about 1.75 times normal focal length when the front element group is removed. Naturally, the bellows must be racked out to accommodate the longer length with a resultant drop in effective lens speed of about 2¹/₂ stops. With the rear element only, convertible lenses tend to be soft at full aperture, but stopped down a couple of stops further, they regain a satisfactory degree of sharpness. The softness wide open makes a nice portrait lens, also, and symmetrical lenses perform well for closeups. While not so bright to focus as an additional, longer optic, mine has more than once saved the day when I have had trouble with perspective.

Since no one lens is the best choice for every shot, you will probably want a camera which accepts different lenses so that you can vary focal lengths. There are many quality cameras in all of the above sizes that offer such a feature, and almost all the larger press and view cameras offer interchangeable lens boards.

In selecting longer-than-normal lenses, you have two choices as a rule — either telephoto types or normal lenses of longer focal length. Telephotos are generally shorter physically than the indicated focal length: a 6" telephoto lens might be only four inches long. They generally have a narrow field of view. Where the lens-to-film position is fixed, as in most 35 mm. and 2¹/₄" square reflexes, such telephoto lenses are fine. However, with the ideal type of still-life camera, one in which the lens can be moved or tilted in relation to the film position, I prefer the normal lenses which give greater coverage. Such lenses are generally less expensive, but be sure that you have sufficient bellows draw to use longer lenses on your camera at close working distances. A 14" lense needs more bellows draw than is normally furnished on many 4" x 5" press or view cameras. To use a 14" lens, working fairly close to small objects, a 22" bellows draw or, better still, a 24" draw is needed. If you do not have enough bellows to handle a long normal lens, a telephoto lens must be your answer.

THE SHUTTER

Chances are that the shutter furnished with any quality lens will provide an adequate shutter for your purposes. There are exceptions, however, and it might be well to note some of the potential problems.

There are two basic types of shutters: the leaf shutter, which opens and closes either in the middle of the lens assembly or behind it; and the focal-plane shutter that draws a slotted curtain across the film close to the film plane. The leaf shutter differentiates speeds by remaining open or closed for a varying period of time while light passes through. A focal-plane shutter varies either the size of the slot traveling across the film or the speed at which the slot travels.

In general, the leaf type, or between-the-lens shutter, as it is often called, is the preferred design for your purposes. The best are durable, and they are easily synchronized to flash. They work without noticeable vibration — very important in long exposure work — and are relatively accurate over long periods of time. The old standby in leaf-type shutters is the Compur. I think I have used dozens of them, some of the old types approaching nearly four decades in age, and have never had one fail me or require more than cleaning.

Shutters, like any mechanical device — and this is a highly precise and complex one — will vary somewhat from the norm, and if you do a lot of color work, it would be well to run some exposure tests with the exposure meter and type of film you use in your work. You may find that you have to make adjustments for a shutter that is running slightly faster than marked, or as is more often the case, slower than the settings say. It is well to check carefully before you buy, for while there are many good brands, there are also some very troublesome ones, and *shutters are expensive to repair*. Cleaning and adjustment on a Compur-type shutter now costs at least eighteen dollars, while focal-plane shutters can cost forty dollars or more for repairs.

The first commercial product photography I did was with a 4" x 5" Graflex that sported a focal-plane shutter; I bought it because it was about the only camera that size I could find for the fifteen dollars I had. The focal-plane shutter has practically disappeared from cameras larger than 35 mm., and I believe for a good reason. They had vibration, repair, synchronization, and adjustment problems. In the 35 mm. single-lens reflex, largely because of the demand for lens interchangeability, I believe, they have remained the predominant type. If you are going to use a focal plane reflex, be sure that you get one that performs at slow speeds with a minimum of vibration.

Slow speeds are the most important ones on any shutter you use in a studio. You will probably use your one-second or half-second setting a hundred times for each time you use even a speed of 1/50. Do not buy a camera or shutter that does not offer you a range of speeds from one second to 1/25. Making a bulb or time exposure is not as accurate as making exposures with shutter-timed speeds, and it is a nuisance. If your shutter did not go above

1/25, lacked all high speeds, as some types of studio camera shutters do, it would probably never bother you a bit. When buying a camera, check these slow speeds. They are not only the ones you will use the most, but they are the speeds at which a malfunction, indicating that a shutter is dirty or in need of repair can most easily be recognized. Sometimes, if a camera has been sitting on a dealer's shelf for a long time, the oil may get gummy and simply working the shutter a few times may correct the problem, but in such cases get a guarantee.

Amateur photographers want synchronization for flash and electronic flash and will often reject shutters and cameras not so equipped. Lenses mounted in shutters which do not offer flash synchronization are generally substantially cheaper. A commercial studio would certainly prefer a synchronized shutter, since they often have legitimate use for flash and electronic flash on assignments. For still-life work flash synchronization is probably of very limited importance, and a good unsynchronized shutter-lens combination can be a great buy. Anything without flash probably dates from before World War II, but I have never known a lens to wear out from the light passing through it.

7. Basic Accessories for the Camera

In addition to lighting equipment, which is treated at length in the next chapter, there are a number of basic accessories which are as important to good pictures as a proper camera. They should be picked with the same care.

THE TRIPOD

If your camera moves during exposure, your pictures will not be sharp. This is especially true in studio work, where you use longer exposure times. The qualifications of a fine tripod are few and easily recognized.

A tripod should be rock solid. The legs and head should lock firmly but permit easy adjustment. A good tripod will allow vertical adjustment to at least six feet and preferably seven feet. The head should allow full adjustment to any angle, including a vertical tilt for copying on the floor. Elevator posts in the center are very handy, but not vital. Geared pan heads are expensive and of limited value to the still-life photographer.

If you use a 4″ x 5″ view camera, a heavy studio stand which is hard to move is probably preferable to a tripod. However, for lighter 4″ x 5″ and smaller cameras, there are many fine portable units. Unfortunately good tripods cost at least forty dollars and few show up secondhand in good condition. A personal favorite is the Tiltall tripod, which I have found adequate for most studio work and reasonably portable for location shooting. Avoid the slick little chrome jobs. They open and close with a flick of the wrist and are light and pretty, but when they wiggle they are little more than works of art, and what you need is a dependable tool.

80

THE SELECTION AND USE OF EXPOSURE METERS

I have seen amateurs who thought they were experienced enough to work without an exposure meter, but I cannot recall that I have ever seen a professional working in his studio without one. Even if you are a single-lens 35 mm. type who is blessed with a built-in meter, you will probably want a hand-held meter to eliminate the necessity of unbolting your camera from the tripod to make a closeup reading.

Meters can be difficult to select. You will find an array of electric types ranging in price from five dollars to well over a hundred dollars. The most expensive instruments generally offer very narrow fields of view, they are spot meters or offer extreme ranges of sensitivity which are not needed in most work. There is a host of good meters in the twenty-five dollar to forty dollar list price range, and many of these are discounted.

Size is one clue to durability and performance. The mini-meters, while convenient, are like tiny watches — they tend to be less rugged and often less reliable in general.

The dial should be easily legible. It should be easy to reset the dial from one film speed to another. Ease in reading is generally aided by a meter with a low light scale and a separate high or bright range. What this does in effect is to expand the low range of a normal scale into a whole range of needle swing, making more accurate readings possible. In some meters, this is accomplished by having a slide that is removable for working at lower light levels, which you do frequently in studio work.

There are two types of power source for meters: the old standby photo-electric cell and the newer cadmium-sulfide type which relies on a battery. The photoelectric meter generates a microvolt current which varies with the amount of light. The CDS meters with a battery depend on the battery as a power source, and a resistance is measured which varies with exposure to varying light levels. In general, the CDS meters have great sensitivity to extremely low light levels, and are of great aid in available-light shooting. Both types of quality instrument are dependable and either will do its job well. My personal preference is the photoelectric type for a couple of basic reasons: I hate to have to depend on and check batteries, and the photoelectric meter reacts almost instantly as you move it across a scene or vary light levels. Some CDS units may have a momentary "memory" before they move accurately. A good photoelectric meter will perform well for many, many years and nothing short of dropping it is likely to throw it off significantly. And I have never found a still-life shooting situation in which I was working nearly in the dark.

When you have made a choice between a CDS or photoelectric meter, you have yet another choice to make. There are two distinctly different categories of meter. One type reads the light reflected by the object or scene; this is, logically, called a reflected light meter. It is pointed at the object being photographed. The second type is called an incident light meter and measures the light falling on the scene. While many better meters of either variety are furnished with accessories which permit them to be used either way, the converted meters are never quite as easy to use in the situation for which they were not designed.

I have found the incident light meter handiest for photographing still-life setups. You can hold the meter at the object being photographed, pointing it back at the camera and lights, and accurately measure the light falling on it. Using the hemispheric cell cover furnished with most such meters, you get an integrated reading from all light sources directed on the subject.

A flat cell cover is a useful accessory for the beginning still-life photographer. By pointing the meter with its flat cell cover in place at each light source you can determine the relative brightness of each light source and mathematically balance the lighting. As you gain in experience, you will dispense with checking the brightness range except where you are using extreme lighting ranges for special effects. If illumination is different on different parts of a scene or setup you are shooting, use a compromise setting halfway between the high and low readings, but in doing so, realize that the scene will not look evenly illuminated. No general set of instructions will cover all meters. *Read the manufacturer's brochure of instructions carefully and follow his instructions with the meter in hand.*

Reflected light meters also work perfectly well in most studio situations if reasonable care is taken. These meters are pointed at the subject, preferably while being held close enough to it to measure the reflected light from only the most important part of the subject. If you are using a backlight, it is likely to be so positioned that much of its light will strike the meter cell directly. This would be similar to shooting a backlighted subject out-of-doors. In such a case, you must either shield a reflected light meter from light which falls directly on it or measure the scene with such highlighting turned off.

Except with a spot meter, which has a very small angle of view, very small objects are likely to throw a reflected light meter off, since most meters measure a scene larger than the object. Here, too, there is a possible, if inconvenient, method of using a reflected light meter. Let us assume you are photographing a small white can, such as a 35 mm. film container, against a dark background. You can place a card or other object of approximately the same color and reflectance in the spot where the can will be and take a meter reading from the larger substitute object. If, however, you generally work with objects of 6″ x 6″ or larger, a good reflected light meter reading can be made by moving the meter in on the subject. Be careful not to block light from any source when doing so.

I generally use my reflected light meter for photography outdoors, but when I do take it into the studio, I am glad it has one feature: an indicator needle lock. Even its good dial is often difficult to read when the light is in front of it. The lock switch lets me carry the meter with the reading to the light for dial adjustment and also "remembers" the reading for me.

The biggest fallacy in meter use is thinking that a meter gives an "answer." It cannot because there is no answer. One person prefers a given scene to look thin and in pastel hues — he will overexpose a color slide. Another will underexpose to get deep colors and dramatic color highlights. Meters measure the illumination (the amount of light in the case of an incident light meter) or the brightness of an object (when reading with a reflected light meter). These give an average, generally acceptable exposure. You still have to think about the effect you want. If you want detail in a dark object, you will have to allow several times the exposure you would give it if you wanted to reduce a dark object to a black mass and pick up detail in a near-white object. A good meter is a necessary guide and provides a needed point of departure for determining correct exposure. It does not replace judgment.

Finally, if you are using a meter built into your camera, you will probably want to remove your camera from its stand and move it close to that part of the subject you wish to render most correctly. In other words, use the whole camera as you would a hand-held meter.

MISCELLANEOUS ACCESSORIES FROM THE VARIETY STORE

Some unlikely objects tucked into a drawer in the studio area or into a case taken on location can prove invaluable to the still-life photographer. Some items I always try to have on hand are: (1) wood spring-type clothespins for clipping diffusion paper over lights, holding background, making stands for small objects, holding light cords, etc.; (2) a tacking stapler, mostly for backgrounds and fastening drapes in place, also useful to place that fastening you need quickly and with one hand; (3) florist's clay, which holds many things in place without fuss and remains workable for long periods; (4) tape — masking tape, especially, and also double-stick Scotch tape; (5) focusing cloth — black corduroy or velvet is fine (eliminating extraneous light makes ground glass focusing easier); (6) china-marking pencils, white and black, for marking the ground glass on a view camera, or anything else you want to be able to rub clean with your finger; (7) a short ladder — 3' will generally reach those high lights, background, and camera; (8) tissues — rolls of white tracing tissue make great diffusers, tents, reflectors, etc., and lens tissues are handy for wiping optical surfaces; (9) foil, which will make masks over a hot light bulb without deteriorating and is a handy reflector since it can be cut or folded for instant sizing; (10) venetian-blind cord, strong enough for most suspension or tieup problems, and coils neatly for reuse; (11) mat knife, for the things that always need trimming and cutting (and you cannot put this one in a pocket and forget it); (12) screw drivers and pliers in a few sizes from very small to normal, since even the most precise equipment, when used hard, may loosen up here and there.

With your first setup and your first problems, you will be adding your own pet hardware to the above.

THE GADGET TRAP

I sometimes suspect that almost all photographers are at heart incurable gadgeteers. There is certainly no harm in indulging one's fancy for exotic widgets if budget and space permit, but one caution is that testing, changing, sorting, storing, and just carrying unneeded doodads can get in the way of the prime object of your activity — making pictures. Just for reference, here is a list of popular accessories, with my comments:

Filters. In black-and-white photography, filters can be used to adjust the relative contrast or emphasis of colors in a multicolored scene as recorded monochromatically. In general, panchromatic films (the most popular type) try to render colors in tones of gray that we would find natural. However, if it is recognized that a filter will pass more light of its own color, while holding back others, possible uses become obvious. If you photograph a light yellow pattern on a white background, a yellow filter will tend to pass more yellow while holding back other parts of the light spectrum as represented in the white background. Similarly, if you photograph a piece of red wood, such as teak, a red filter will tend to increase the grain pattern of the wood in the final result. When the basic problems have been mastered, some study of filters and their uses in relationship to specific films can add a dimension of control to your work.

In color photography you can see, by looking through a colored glass filter, pretty much what it will do to a photograph of a scene. A blue filter will tend to cool colors, an orange filter will warm them. Special effects can be obtained in color with filters. Furthermore, different types of light sources will have different color temperatures that require filtration (see Chapter 3).

The polarizing filter is a useful one for many studio problems. This filter tends to reduce or eliminate unwanted highlights caused by nonmetallic reflection. The results are visible in use with any camera where you view the subject through the lens and can sometimes solve some sticky reflection and "hot spot" problems.

Filters generally change the exposure. Read carefully the instructions that come packed with film and filters regarding exposure changes. To adjust exposure for filters (compensate for filter factors) one of the easiest things to do is to cut the film speed setting on the meter by the factor. For example, if you are using a film rated at 100 A.S.A. with a filter requiring a factor of 2, you would set the film speed at 50; with a factor of 4, set it at 25, etc.

Cable release. You have to have one. Its purpose is simply to reduce vibration when you trip the shutter and thus cut down camera movement. The flexible, fabric-covered types are generally more satisfactory than the more

84

heavily armored types for slow speed shooting, since they transmit less hand movement. Get one long enough for you to work comfortably away from your camera. In an emergency, a built-in self-timer can be used to trip the shutter without vibration.

Closeup devices. All closeup devices tend to move the lens away from the film, or, in the case of supplementary lenses, to shorten the focal length of the lens optically. In order of flexibility, they might be shown as: adjustable bellows, adjustable extension tubes, extension tube sets in many forms, and proxar supplementary lenses, which come in varying strengths for varying distance ranges.

These are substitutes for the right equipment in the first place. A camera with a long bellows as part of its basic design or, in miniatures, a properly designed close-focusing mount with a macrolens computed for closeup work are the best answers.

Copying stands are also very appealing pieces of engineering, but if you only occasionally find yourself doing copy work, use your good tripod as a stand.

Auxiliary lenses purportedly convert normal lenses into wide-angle and telephoto optics and cost a fraction of the real thing. Don't believe it! They do what they say, but generally with an unacceptable degree of quality deterioration in the image. There are such specialized lenses for the Rolleiflex cameras that reportedly do a fine job, but they are priced well above the twenty- to forty-dollar magical sets! Test before buying!

Lens hoods (sunshades) are a must! Be sure that the shade is not so wide that it does not effectively shield the lens from extraneous light, and not so narrow, on a wide-angle lens, that it will vignette the image the lens produces.

A summary of junk. Good photographs are generally produced by good skills and practice and quality basic equipment and lights. It is seldom that a new gadget will improve the result. The myriad offerings seen in the photographic magazines, including optical or color screens, trick viewfinders, supplementary lenses to do anything to a lens except what it was designed to do, "bargain" meters and lenses, trick flash devices, handgrips, trick "pods," and the other gadgets that imply they are supplements to skill, are more likely to supply clutter than convenience. Buy very selectively and, as with basic equipment, buy quality.

DARKROOM EQUIPMENT

This text does not treat any matters of film processing or printing simply because they are parts of an exacting art-science which the majority of serious photographers often leave to professional laboratories. However, in considering equipment for picture-making beyond the camera itself, it must be said that a darkroom of your own will give you significantly greater control over your results than outside finishing of even the best type, and can save a considerable amount of money.

You can get into darkroom work by stages, too. Start with a developing tank, a thermometer, and a few chemicals to process your own film — this will involve a total investment of perhaps ten to fifteen dollars — and later become more ambitious, moving on to enlarging, retouching, and color printing.

In any event, the minimum darkroom equipment any photographer must consider is some good how-to-do-it books on the subject. Until you know the methods by which your pictures will be processed, and their limitations, your equipment as a picture-taker is not complete. Just knowing what the man in the darkroom can and must do will give you great insight into exposing and lighting a picture.

8. Light and Lighting Equipment

Nearly twenty years ago I was assigned the job of supervising the obtaining of photographs for the large home furnishing and giftware firm by which I was employed. I had been fascinated with photography and cameras since before I was old enough to become a Boy Scout, and this was a welcome assignment that went on for many years. Every few months we made literally hundreds of photographs for our catalogs, salesmen's kits, and publicity. The men and studios who made these photographs for us were excellent teachers. One of the best was Tom Anton of New York City. Tom seemed to have infinite patience (a prime qualification for a still-life photographer), and one of his greatest talents as a photographer was his ability to keep equipment simple — especially lighting. He once told me, "There is no subject that requires more than three lights." On location he would often come to the job with only three or four lights, and his results were first-rate. In the studio, in addition to basic lighting, he would have the luxury of additional lamps or conveniently mounted reflectors to help add highlights or more easily manipulate light quality, but his lighting setups were always basic and logical. And even when he worked with few lights, we rejected very few photographs. In subsequent years of shooting sessions at other studios, batteries of lighting equipment were also available, but I noted that the best photographers kept their lighting uncomplicated.

A great variety of lighting equipment is required by the commercial photographer because he must shoot a great variety of subjects, each a different problem in visual quality and scale. The professional's time is money, and if he has the best light at hand for a setup to shoot a diamond ring, and can then pull it away and bring up the proper lights on the next set to shoot a room full of furniture, he saves time. You will probably require only a few lights to handle only your particular kind of subject.

A great many reflectors, light stands and tables, diffusing screens, and reflectors I have seen in use professionally were made because the photographer found a need and built his own solution. Circles of plywood with several simple aluminum reflectors bolted onto them, light boxes with bulbs inside and diffusing glass above, sheets of board with crinkled aluminum foil, others painted matte white or aluminum to use as reflectors can be fitted with connectors to mount on light stands. Small mirrors glued to blocks of wood, placed behind objects on a table to redirect light to other objects in complex table-top arrangements, can be handy. The basic lights, of course, were always durable, wired with heavy-duty cords, and kept clean and in good working order.

SOURCES OF LIGHT

Daylight

The source of light we learn about first, and seldom even observe, is the sun. It dominates our thinking, however, in almost all artificial lighting problems, and in many ways the effects you work to achieve in the studio are a simulation of light outdoors. For example, in any artificial setup you will have one dominant light, and, with very rare exceptions, will limit yourself to a single visible shadow. People are so conditioned by the single light source that two or more shadows in a photograph may disturb and disorient them, although they will not realize why they are bothered.

If you have ever taken pictures of people on the beach, you know how pleasing and brilliant the results can be. The sun is a great main light, and the sand, a fine reflector, will bounce light to fill in the shadow areas. The use of a main light plus reflector will solve many in-studio problems.

I have often gone outside to make product shots, especially in a situation where an outdoor background, either because it carried a message or added visual interest, was indicated by the subject. It can work wonderfully well, but it can also be a problem. While you can move an object somewhat in relation to the sun, you cannot move the sun as you would a studio lamp. In other words, out of doors you have only limited control over the intensity and position of your light source. That is the principal reason for working indoors.

Almost as much equipment may be needed for an outdoor shooting session as you would require in a studio. No lights are needed, of course, except possibly a portable electronic flash or flashbulb for fill-in illumination, but you will need reflectors (often no more than white cardboards with sticks for props). Large diffusing screens covered with wire screening (aluminum or white sprayed) or scrim (a light mesh fabric) can also be very helpful to diffuse sunlight. The reflectors can help you catch sunlight and redirect it into shadow areas. The intensity of the fill-in light reflected can be controlled by the proximity of the reflector to the subject. The quality of reflected light can be controlled by the nature of the reflecting material. Shiny smooth aluminum wrap laminated to a board will produce a different kind of light than the same material crinkled. The reflectors you must use outside can also serve when you photograph indoors. They should be mounted so that they allow some adjustment without moving the stands on which they are mounted. A variety of inexpensive ball-and-socket joints are sold in photographic supply stores for mounting lamps and for use on tripods as tiltheads. These can easily be adapted to reflector board mounts.

You do have choices in outdoor lighting. Early in the morning and late in the day you will have strongly directional light that picks up texture and throws long, dramatic shadows. Between 10:00 and 11:00 A.M. and between about 2:00 and 3:00 P.M. you have perhaps the most normal and useful light: a high, clear, but still somewhat directional sun. On clear days the light is strong and clean in color. Subjects are brilliant. However, an overcast day offers a diffused light that is lovely for pictures requiring a soft quality and, if you are shooting in color, it is good light for achieving soft, almost pastel, tones. Once you start thinking about photographing objects out-of-doors, you will begin to observe how things look in different light and you can plan the time and location of your photographs.

The light out-of-doors can give you some problems, however. A few of the pitfalls are worth noting before you start.

(1) When using your meter, move in close to the subject. The light around it — extraneous light reflected from the background — may throw an exposure reading way off. Decide in contrasty light situations whether you are most interested in recording the shadow areas with detail, or the highlights. Take your exposure reading on the area of most interest.

(2) Do not use high speed black-and-white films outside. For example, outside you may want to shoot with a lens wide open or nearly wide open to reduce your depth of field and throw disturbing background out of focus. With fast film in your camera, and a top shutter speed of 1/250 on your shutter, in normal daylight you would be forced to keep your lens stopped down to f/11, f/16 or less. You would have quite a bit of depth of field, which might well keep backgrounds much more in evidence than you like. With a slower film, such as Kodak's Panatomic-X (A.S.A. 40), you could shoot at f/5.6, cutting down the depth of field considerably. This is less of a problem with color films, since they are generally slower, but again, avoid high-speed color materials.

(3) Your equipment, and especially your film, must be kept cool. Heat can do a lot of unexpected things, such as ruining a film emulsion or melting the cement that holds lens elements together. Black "professional" camera finishes are much in vogue today. Black metal heats faster than chrome. Pick a shady spot for your gear on warm days. While I have never found it very attractive to photograph objects outside on cold winter days, if you are tempted, keep your shutters warm — perhaps in an inside pocket. They tend

to slow down when lubricants congeal. Similarly, cold objects stored in an air-conditioned room taken out on a warm, humid day can produce condensation on film and lenses.

(4) Shooting in the shade can, like shooting on an overcast day, provide very desirable indirect light for certain types of subjects. This is fine if you are shooting black-and-white, but be cautious if you have color film in your camera. Light filtering through leaves or reflected from a green lawn is likely to be green, as noted earlier. Your eye adjusts to cancel the green out, but a photographic film will not make that adjustment. Reflected light is reflected as colored light when reflected by a colored surface to an extent that your subject will be discolored. Of course, in looking for special effects, a colored reflecting surface can produce some interesting results.

(5) In early morning and late afternoon, sunlight has a strong reddish hue. Fine, if that is what you want, but if you are shooting for color accuracy, you would do best to photograph between 10:00 A.M. and 4:00 P.M.

3200° K. Tungsten Lighting

Tungsten bulbs are, in my opinion, the most useful type of still-life studio lighting. Most bulbs are comparatively inexpensive to replace. The equipment used to hold them starts at two or three dollars for simple spun-aluminum reflectors and ranges to higher but still very reasonable prices for more durable and convenient lighting units. Their characteristic bulb life of fifteen to sixty hours, depending on the type of bulb, is reasonable, and they have a high degree of color temperature stability for over two-thirds of their working life.

Almost every type of lighting unit you might require will accept 3200°K. bulbs, and bulbs can be purchased in most good electrical supply stores and photographic supply outlets servicing the professional trade. You can thus match color temperatures of a 150-watt baby spotlight, a 500-watt spotlight and floodlamps easily. For the do-it-yourself light builder, tungsten bulbs will fit standard household sockets, although porcelain sockets are a good investment because of the heat developed by the high wattages.

A wide variety of transparency and negative color film are available balanced for 3400°K. lighting, and any film balanced for 3400°K. can be used successfully with 3200° lights by slipping an 81A filter over the camera lens. Good results can be obtained even without filtration, though a conversion filter does increase color accuracy.

Perhaps the most important advantage to 3200°K. tungsten lighting over other types is that you can arrange, adjust, and observe your lighting with such units. The light stays on while you create the effect you want. The trouble you take with the arrangement of your lighting will have a greater effect on the resulting photographs than anything else you do. The wide degree of control that can be obtained with tungsten light recommends it as a studio standard.

When shooting only black-and-white, considerations of color temperature are of little importance, but the flexibility of tungsten lighting is still a desirable feature. Since you never know when you will want to shoot color, I have found it a good idea to standardize on bulbs of one temperature, 3200°K.

With any tungsten lighting there are a few problems to anticipate. The first is, how many lamps can you plug into a line before you blow a fuse? Most home or office circuits are fused for either 15 or 20 amperes and occasionally for 30 amperes, Most operate at 115, 120, or 125 volts (check your current to be sure you buy bulbs of proper voltage). Since a watt equals one ampere times one volt, if you multiply the fused amperage in your location by the operating voltage, the product will be in watts. For example, if you have house current of 120 volts and are fused for 20 amperes, a line should carry 2400 watts. If you are using over 2400 watts, you had best plug some of your lamps into a second *line* (not a second *outlet*). To keep accurate color temperatures, it is best to keep somewhat less wattage than the maximum possible on a single line. For the same reason, try to plug into heavy-duty wall outlets, or split your lamps up among several outlets. When you use extension cords, get heavy ones which will not severely restrict the flow of current and cause your lamps to burn at less than peak efficiency.

For extremely critical work, the voltage should be checked at the bulb with a voltmeter. Various devices— most quite expensive — can be purchased to maintain constant voltages, but unless power is noticeably deficient in your building, this is unnecessary. Color temperature variations of 100°K. with transparency films are hardly noticeable with normal subjects; and a variation of 100°K. would require a voltage fluctuation of 10 volts with household lamps.

Photographic Flood Lamps

The type of photographic lamp sold in the drugstore-type photography counters is not suitable for serious work and should be used only in an emergency. Their initial color temperature of 3400°K. changes rapidly over their fairly short life of six hours or less.

Quartz-Iodine Lamps

In special cases, these may be your answer. They are easily the most appealing in design. For the light produced, they offer the most portable a.c. light source and have, compared to other types of tungsten lamps, a very long life — from 16 to 150 hours — with little change in color temperature during the bulb life. However, they are extremely concentrated light sources and throw a harsh light which may have to be diffused. Like other concentrated lighting, they can be excellent for bounce-light work.

One of their greatest faults, in my experience, is that they are not generally available in a wide variety of reflector of spotlighting units. Smith Victor and other firms do make adaptors so that they may be used in standard sockets, but their light quality is still quite different from tungsten bulbs. But if much of your work is on location or you have to pack away your equipment after use, they are well worth checking. Smith Victor makes a beautiful studio kit which packs away, stands and all, in a slick and light attaché case. Since they are available in both 3200°K. and 3400°K. color temperatures, quartz-iodine lamps can be combined with professional lighting units of identical color temperatures. General Electric and Sylvania also make this type of lamp.

Electronic Flash

The electronic flash is the type of artificial light which most closely resembles daylight in color quality. In general, electronic flash units produce a flash of very short duration, 1/500 of a second or less. When exposing color film, this very short burst of light can cause a color shift and effect a change in color balance. However, as a practical matter, even a small electronic flash unit can work well out-of-doors as fill-in illumination. This technique is generally referred to as synchro-sunlight.

To balance daylight with your flash outside, you must calculate a flash exposure which equals your daylight exposure as indicated by your meter. Note that the effect of each light source on exposure is controlled by different factors:

Flash	Daylight
flash-to-subject distance	lens aperture
aperture of lens	shutter speed
If flash duration is less than duration of exposure, the shutter setting makes no difference.	Shutter speed can be changed without affecting exposure value of electronic flash.

As a procedure: (1) read your meter for proper daylight exposure; (2) set your lens/shutter according to meter reading; (3) know the guide number of your flash unit from the manufacturer's instruction guide or from the flash-bulb package; (4) divide the f stop you are using into the guide number for the correct lamp-to-subject distance.

For example, let us assume that you have a flash, which, with the film you are using, has a guide number of 40. (The guide number equals flash-to-subject distance multiplied by lens aperture.) Convenience indicates that

92

you should place your flash five feet from the subject. Dividing the distance into the guide number gives us an aperture of f/8. That is, disregarding the daylight, with flash only, you would expose at f/8. Let us further assume that it is a bright day and your meter tells you that the daylight indicates possible exposures between f/5.6 at 1/250 of a second and f/16 at 1/25 of a second. We know you must expose at f/8 because of the flash, you would then set your shutter at 1/100, the indicated speed to give you a correct daylight exposure at an aperture of f/8.

The result will be something approaching flat lighting. If you wish to favor the highlights produced by the daylight, you would reduce the amount of light from the flash by moving the flash farther away. With a guide number of 40, a move from a distance of five feet to about seven feet will about cut the light in half, giving you a lighting ratio of one (for daylight) to two (for flash illumination). We know this because whereas your original calculation for the flash exposure indicated an aperture of f/8, with the flash at seven feet, the formula works out to $\frac{40 \text{ (guide number)}}{7 \text{ (flash-to-subject distance)}}$ = approximately f/5.6, or one stop more. This indicates that for proper exposure, you should set your camera at f/5.6, but by leaving it at f/8 you are giving 50 percent less light to the shadow areas. Similarly, you can move the flash in, cut down on lens aperture, and treat daylight as a fill-in. This tends to underexpose the background and, for that reason, is a frequently used trick of press photographers who do not want to have a confusing background interfere with their subject.

For studio work, the small amateur-type electronic flash units, even used in multiples, are hardly satisfactory for photographing objects. You cannot see the light on your subject until you develop your negative. This eliminates any possibility of adjusting the lights creatively before shooting and visualizing the results as you work. Also, flash units produce a limited amount of light and are suitable for small setups only. Perhaps there is an occasional bounce flash setup where an electronic flash would help to solve a problem.

Big electronic studio flash units are expensive. A decent installation with multiple-flash heads can easily cost more than a thousand dollars. Such units are inexpensive to operate in terms of electrical current and will stop action when a photographer is working with live models in a large studio, but I have never found them to be good working lights for product photography. Even units with modeling lights produce a light on the subject quite different from what you see on your negative. Furthermore, the effect of an electronic flash is far less predictable than other types of light sources in switching from one film emulsion to another. Tests must be run before shooting a job. The one situation I recall when I was glad to have a set of electronic flash units in the studio was when photographing a group of hanging mobiles. Perhaps you should let a professional photographer take those shots for you. It is cheaper than buying the equipment. Or take your subject outside in daylight if it moves; use a high shutter speed and pretend that the background is what you wanted all along.

Flashbulbs

I cannot recall when I have used flashbulbs for a product photograph except outdoors to balance daylight, as previously described. They can produce a little or a lot of light, depending on the bulb you choose; they are cheap and can be used in inexpensive equipment, and they are highly portable and versatile in that you can easily carry bulbs of various sizes for different needs.

Flashbulbs come in clear and blue-coated versions. The blue ones approximate daylight and are the ones to have around, since they can be used with either color or black-and-white film.

A single bulb pointed at the subject, when not balanced by daylight, can produce harsh results and disturbing shadows. With the flashgun held a few feet away from the camera, results on a closeup improve, but are still not great. Bounced off a wall or ceiling, a single bulb produces more natural results but you must increase exposure. Use a light-to-subject distance by estimating the distance from the bulb to the reflecting surface to the subject being photographed and then open a stop or two wider than that indicated by the guide number formula.

Multiple flash will produce better results since, with two or three reflectors loaded with flashbulbs, you can approximate standard portrait or studio lighting setups. The relative brightness of each source can be varied by adjusting the light-to-subject distance. Remember, light diminishes by the square of the distance; one light twice as far away as another in similar reflectors will give you one quarter the light on the subject, not one-half. This produces a one-to-four brightness ratio in the areas illuminated by each.

Flashbulbs should then be considered emergency lights, a light source for photographs including people-plus-object or object-plus-interior, but should not be considered as a prime tool for still-life work.

Fluorescent Lamps

Fluorescent lamps are a poor choice as a light source for product photography. Directional lighting and control of intensity of balance are difficult to achieve with them. Even with sophisticated equipment and a high degree of technical knowledge, they are always to be avoided in color photography. If you are stuck with fluorescents as a light source on a location job, especially in color, check one of the listed publications for technical and filtration information.

DO NOT MIX LIGHT SOURCES
OF DIFFERENT COLOR TEMPERATURES

You will remember the day you shoot your first batch of color work in a room well lit by daylight using artificial illumination on your subject. The human eye adapts for changes in the color of familiar types of light sources. We see color somewhat subjectively. The implacable emulsion of a color film cannot adjust. With an indoor film, everything the daylight illuminates will have a bluish cast, where the highlights produced by your artificial lighting would appear normal.

You cannot correct this type of situation by filters, either, since a filter will change all colors equally. If you balance down the blue daylight to your indoor film, the artificially illuminated areas will appear unnaturally orange. Any daylight illumination has to be kept to a negligible level or eliminated. Dark shades are essential in a room normally used as a photographic studio during daylight hours. For occasional work, schedule shooting at night or shoot in a space without windows.

CHOOSING THE PROPER LIGHTING EQUIPMENT

The equipment you need depends largely on the type of subject you are going to photograph. As you select your lights and stands you will be concerned with the following:

The quantity of light. Large subjects require more light than small ones in order to be illuminated to a comfortable working level. About 500 footcandles of main light illumination on the subject is, I feel, the minimum for color work.

Control of light direction. Reflectors and stands with easily manipulated swivels and firm locks are a first consideration. Devices such as barn doors and snoots which help mask out unwanted light are most useful.

Barn doors, which allow you to shield the camera lens from extraneous light to control the mood and density of highlights and shadows and help prevent the spillage of light onto the parts of your subject, are available for most reflectors, and should be provided for each, or for at least each two, basic reflector units and for each spotlight. Snoots are similar light masks that allow spots of light to pass while holding back unwanted light. They are essentially inverted funnels and can be easily improvised with some cardboard, tape, and clothespins when they are needed. For the permanent working studio, commercial models fitted to your lights are, naturally, more convenient. For the most precise control of the direction and intensity of a light beam, you will need a spotlight or two with good Fresnel lenses and focusing controls.

Light quality control. Diffusers which clip on securely fitted to your reflectors are useful for softening light. A sheet of tracing tissue with some clothespins to hold it in place will work as well as a diffuser.

Tungsten reflectors vary in the size of the bulb they will accommodate and in the angle of the light beam they throw. If you are shooting large subjects and your working space is restricted, you will want reflectors that spread light rapidly. Such reflectors will have a beam of at least 60° and perhaps as much as 100°. Conversely, if you want greater control of your light for smaller subjects, you will need lights which produce beams of 40° or spotlights which can be narrowed still more.

Quality reflectors that have sturdy swivel mounts and good porcelain or phenolic sockets and are mounted on solid stands that will extend to ceiling height offer great convenience and save a lot of burned fingers. It is always helpful for carrying and storage if your equipment nests to some extent.

If you have the luxury of permanent studio space where you can leave lights on their own stands, wire light switches right into the stands. Almost invariably the switches provided on cords are somewhere other than where you want them when you reach for them, and those that operate directly on the light socket are, in most cases, among the hottest things devised by man.

Some typical lighting units are shown in an appendix. Others vary in price from a few dollars to over four figures per unit. The Smith Victor Corporation makes a wide assortment of good lights, stands, and accessories at reasonable prices and will provide catalogs upon request.

9. Lighting Problems and Solutions

Light is the crucial element in photography. Meters measure it, lenses direct it, film records it. Everything you do in making a photograph involves the capturing of reflected light. It naturally follows that in trying to reproduce the image of a subject, setting up the correct lighting is the most important single thing you can do. Care spent in lighting your subject will eliminate most of the problems that may be encountered later as you proceed toward the making of a final print or transparency.

In setting up lights, we are concerned with quantity of light, quality of light, direction of light, and shadows, or the blocking of light. We are also concerned with the balancing of two or more sources of light.

In setting up examples, it must be noted that no two objects are identical and that, therefore, no two subjects will require exactly the same lighting setup. The diagrams and examples included here are intended to give the photographer who is new to still-life photography a point of departure in tackling a lighting problem. You know how you want to present your subject, and you should strive to show an object as you see it in your own mind's eye. There are no formulas for lighting all objects. The objective of your own efforts should be to develop your own visual solutions.

In the previous chapter I discussed the simulation of natural, outdoor lighting as a desirable objective in the studio. This has certain natural corollaries in setting your lights: (1) Your main light, like the sun, should be high, about 40° to 60° above your subject. (2) One sun makes one shadow; so should your lights. (3) Outdoor surfaces generally bounce around enough sunlight to illuminate details in the shadows. Your secondary, or fill-in, lights and reflectors have this function. (4) Bounce lighting is directionless lighting, the studio counterpart of an overcast day. It is a most helpful technique, but unless you like looking at everything under overcast skies, it is not a universal answer.

97

There is another important consideration in determining lighting direction in the studio. Our eyes are *two* lenses. We perceive depth stereoscopically. If you were to walk around with only one eye open, your impression of objects would be more like those you get with your camera. Your perception of the depth of an object would be determined by shadows and shading on that object. With direct front lighting, shadows and shadings tend to disappear, and the objects seen with one eye start to flatten out. You will find that moving a main light to the rear of most subjects will add roundness and depth to them. It will also help you separate the tones of the subject from those of the background. Therefore, most often you will find that a product shot should start with a main light to the rear of the subject and then one or more fill-in lights in front of the subject.

LIGHTING, STEP BY STEP

First, a main light should be placed to define the principal shape and contours of the subject. Then add a fill-in light to illuminate the details lost in the shadow areas. Be careful to keep your fill-in weak enough to allow the main light to predominate. Then, add additional lights either to illuminate other planes or areas not adequately illuminated by the first two, or, add those lamps you need to place reflected highlights on the subject where you want them.

Highlights are generally considered an interference in photographing a reflective object. However, they can also do exactly what their name implies — they can highlight a particular angle or plane of an object and tell the viewer a good deal about the surface texture of an object. Once one very simple fact is remembered, you can put highlights where you want them. Light, like a ball, will bounce off a surface at the same angle it hits that surface — "the angle of incidence equals the angle of reflection." Therefore, if you position a small light where the camera lens will be and point it at your subject, and you move around your subject until your eye sees the highlight where you want it to be, your problem is solved. Simply place the light at the point where you view the desired highlight, and the highlight will then appear in the photograph exactly where you want it. Also remember that a reflective object will reflect a large light source as a large highlight; a small light source will be reflected as a point of light. You can obtain linear highlights by masking a light with barn doors or cardboard and allowing the lamp to emit a linear line of light. As you move a large light source like a floodlight farther away, it becomes smaller. When using highlights, position them immediately after your main light is positioned and use fill-in lights afterwards.

One of the most troublesome problems with fill-in lighting is that these lamps create shadows of their own. One way to avoid this problem without reducing the light level unduly by diffusing your fill-in lights too much or placing them too far away is to keep fill-in lighting low. I have often found myself placing a second spotlight below the actual table level and shining it up to illuminate an object.

The number of possible solutions and lights that can be employed in lighting a subject is almost without limit. The examples given here presuppose that you have acquired a limited battery of lighting equipment and that you will wish to use as few lights as possible. As you gain experience, you will want to add equipment to fill your specific needs.

PHOTOGRAPHING PRODUCTS OUTDOORS

Photographing outdoors can provide interesting settings and allow the product photographer to operate without lighting equipment. Reflectors and large diffusing screens (old house screens sprayed white or with mesh replaced by cheesecloth) are helpful tools.

A rough stone wall and weathered picnic table provided a setting for a group photograph of casual cook-and-serve cast-iron cookware. The sun, high and to the left of the camera, provided clear modeling on the objects and was sufficiently high to show distinct texture on the wall behind. Props—vegetable and herbs—suggest the gourmet.

Left:
This photograph was made for a brochure to introduce a new group of pottery serving accessories which were designed with a chicken motif. The stoneware quality of the objects was implied by a rough rock background. The eggs provide scale. The scene was photographed in hazy sunlight with a scrim screen above the subject to further diffuse the light.

Below:
Rough Italian pottery smoking accessories were photographed on the boards of a weathered dock in bright early-afternoon summer sunlight. The vignette effect at the top of the photograph was obtained by shifting a normal 6″ lens off-center on a 4″ x 5″ view camera so that the edge of the circle of illumination projected by the lens on to the film was exceeded.

An ice storm provided an opportunity to photograph silver jewelry out-of-doors (top left). The lens, when stopped down, provided too much depth of field and introduced confusing branch background. By opening the diaphragm of the lens, the background was thrown out of focus and reduced to indistinct highlights (see top right photograph). The branches provide an interesting geometric background for a close-up of the silver pendant (bottom).

This silver bracelet was photographed while the morning sun, low and behind the subject, was still diffused by morning haze. A reflector, held by an assistant, was helpful in providing fill-in illumination and a white surface for the metal to reflect (see setup photo below). The same reflector technique was used to make photographs of the silver pendant on page 101.

USING BOUNCE LIGHT

Bounce light is nearly directionless lighting which approximates the light outdoors on a heavily overcast day. It is fast lighting under which to work in making a series of shots since subjects can be placed in position one after the other without moving the lights. It will handle almost any type of three-dimensional subject, but not necessarily to best advantage. For record photography, it is an excellent solution to working rapidly, since only clarity and identifiable detail are required. Compare these photographs with those that follow illustrating some of the same subjects illuminated by directional lighting.

This African bronze sculpture is well illuminated by bounce light. The detail is clear and no shadows confuse the subject. Much of the material's quality is lost, however, and the photograph lacks dramatic impact. It is an excellent record treatment, perhaps, but hardly enticing as a sales photograph, in contrast to the versions made with direct lighting.

A stoneware vase is clearly defined by bounce light. Would it be more attractive if seen under shape-defining directional light? How large is it? See photograph below with prop leaves.

This plastic juice squeezer presents a problem: with directional lighting to define and separate the white background from the white top, definition is poor. Had a darker background been used, it would have tended to merge with the orange base container.

With the camera position elevated to show the round top, the back was swung on its vertical axis, parallel to the principal plane of the subject. The front element of the convertible Symmar lens was removed to increase its focal length from approximately 4″ to 7″, and distortion was reduced by placing the camera farther from the subject.

104

Bounce lighting of a different type was used for this photograph. Instead of being photographed in a setup such as that shown in the diagram, the entire white room was illuminated with lights bounced off the ceiling and white no-seam paper on the floor. The particular features to be illustrated in this photograph were the compartmented oak drawers and the Formica serving surface. The spoons in the drawer indicate scale. Often, when large pieces cannot be transported to a studio and limited lighting is available on location, bounce light is the only practical answer. Note that the lighting, in this case incandescent floods, could have been replaced in this photograph by bounced flash or electronic flash.

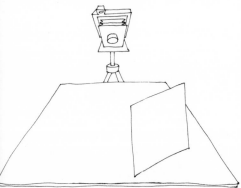

Shadows would destroy a closely packed subject such as this one. Yet some directional lighting was needed to show contours of the wood sculptures. A table covered with light gray no-seam provided a background. The figures were arranged, and sawdust and wood shavings scattered on the table. High windows behind the camera provided the basic illumination. A foil reflector on 30″ x 40″ cardboard was held high and to the left of the subject. The spotlight effect on the background was achieved by burning in the top of the print during enlarging. The camera was a 4″ x 5″ Eastman view camera, and the exposure was made on Tri-X film.

105

DIRECTIONAL LIGHTING

Most products and materials are most aptly handled by directional lighting. The primary tools for lighting control are floodlights with either clear or frosted bulbs, spotlights, reflectors, and occasionally mirrors or mirror-like surfaces such as foil on cardboard. To control the degree of light diffusion or the lack of it, commercial diffusers or white tracing tissue fastened with wooden clothespins can be used over floodlights. To increase the degree to which a spotlight throws parallel rays of light on a subject, snoots can be placed in front of the Fresnel lens of the spotlights. Lights directing strong, nearly parallel rays at the subject will throw distinct, sharply defined shadows, whereas diffuse light sources will create less well-defined shadow outlines.

Directional light can be manipulated to define shape, separate subject from background, pick up texture, and separate the planes of a subject. It is this property of being manipulable that suggests the use of controlled directional lighting in photographing most objects in the studio.

Before setting your lights observe your subject carefully and determine, as clearly as you can, what it is you wish to explain about the object before the camera.

106

This closer view reveals much of the detail of the subject but lacks the interest of a color photograph. See setup and photographs on pages 38 and 39.

107

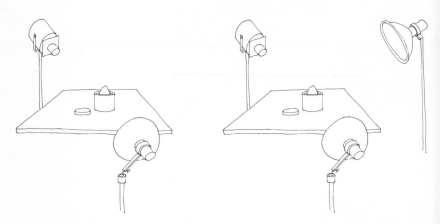

Above left:
A single spotlight with a broad snoot defines the contours of the juicer and shows the translucent nature of the plastic material. The spotlight is placed to "snap out" the juicer and subdue the auxiliary strainer. The white no-seam background goes dark except where the circle of light produced by the spotlight hits it. Foreground detail is hidden in shadow.

Above right:
A diffused floodlight to the right front of the camera provides fill-in for shadows. Some of the dramatic effect of single spotlight lighting is lost, but the objects are clearly defined. Note that the background is lightened by use of fill-in illumination. The white no-seam acts as an additional reflector. For this photograph the camera back was vertical, and the lens board was tilted for maximum depth of field.

108

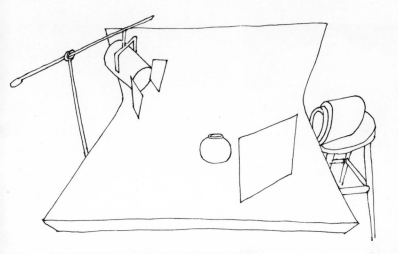

To add roundness to this subject, two equal spotlights were used to the rear and to either side of the vase. While the left-hand spotlight was kept high to illuminate the top, the spotlight to the right had to be kept very low to avoid double shadow. A white matte reflector was used to the right front of the subject to fill shadows. Compare this with the bounce-lighted photograph on page 104. The leaves suggest use and add scale. It is not necessary to show texture in all areas of the subject since it is clearly defined in two areas.

109

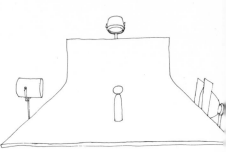

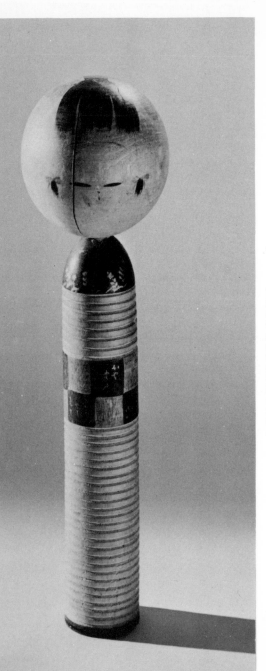

Two problems in roundness are illustrated by this Kokeshi doll. The spherical head required a highlight (top right) to define it. This was provided by a low-power baby spotlight behind the subject and placed high. The combination of a spotlight to the left and a diffused flood lamp to the right provided sufficient modeling for the cylindrical base. Barn doors were used on the floodlamp to restrict the light to the subject and keep the background in shadow. The lighting ratio between the spotlight and floodlamp was 2:1. The camera back was vertical. Compare with the color photograph of the same subject on page 40.

110

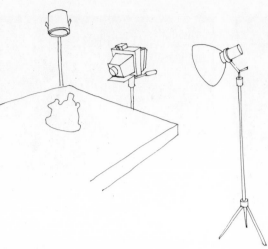

A portrait-like lighting formula was applied here with modification. A spotlight to the right of the camera defines features and crosslights the texture of the bronze. A fill-in floodlamp to the left of the camera softens the shadows. In comparing this to the bounce-lighted photograph of the same object on page 103, note that the detail and character of materials are superior under direct lighting, but that this is done at the price of casting certain parts of the figure into shadow. The lighting ratio was 3:1.

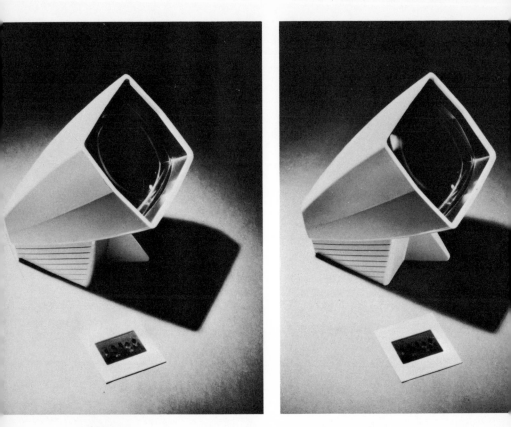

Above left:
Lights must be observed one by one as a lighting setup is arranged. The spotlight alone illuminates this first photograph. It is placed high above the table to illuminate the top and front frame of the viewer. An inexpensive Victor boom easily held the 500-watt spotlight in position. The spotlight was then moved forward to brush the front side of the viewer and provide the modeling on the side of the viewer. A light no-seam background was used to reflect into the shadows. The slide shows the scale of the viewer.

Above right:
Here a second light was added, a diffused floodlamp well below camera height. This not only filled the shadows, but also added definitive highlights on the viewing lens and the edge of the front plane of the viewer.

112

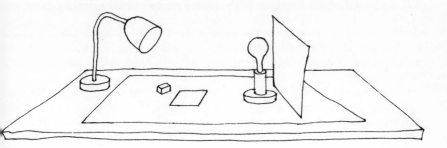

This photograph, intended for use in a promotional mailing piece, was made with improvised emergency lighting. The main light was provided by a flexible desk lamp with a 100-watt bulb "stepped up" by compounding the filament. This is done by letting a household bulb get hot and then tapping it lightly but sharply on a table. The filament is pushed together and several minutes of high-intensity light are available. This main light was used to the left of the camera behind the subject. To the right, another 100-watt bulb, closer to the subject, was intensified by placing a white cardboard behind it. The slight double shadows which resulted were lost in printing.

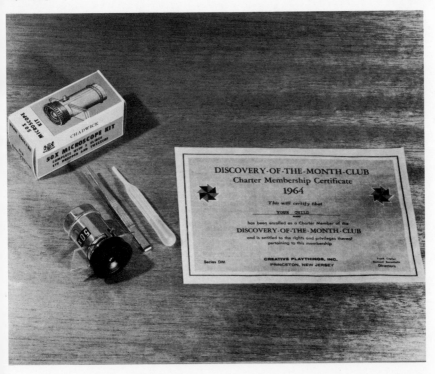

TRANSLUCENT AND TRANSPARENT MATERIALS

The problem in photographing objects of glass or clear plastic is how to take a picture of something you can see through. Such objects should generally be photographed with light transmitted through them rather than with light falling on them.

Fortunately, most transparent objects have clearly defined edges and vary (from the camera angle) in thickness as the edges of objects are reached. Thicker portions tend to transmit less light and it is such variances in the degree of light transmission that are exploited in transillumination.

Faceted or carved glass or plastic can sometimes use direct light to advantage. A few possible points of departure are shown in the following photographs.

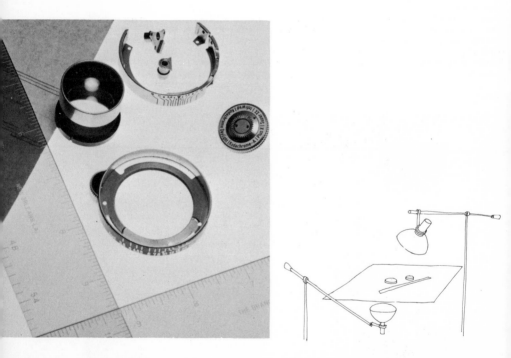

The idea of this photograph is precision. The inclusion of the measuring scale and the blue-print not only add color interest but also impart the idea of engineering without immediate resort to copy. Also note that the simple geometric design helps to highlight the metal parts of the subject.
These objects were shot on a translucent light table, thus eliminating all shadows. A ceiling of light was provided by a large diffused floodlight directly above the subject. While a similar effect with the bright metal parts might have been achieved by tenting, the technique used here sharply defines the various machined details of the metal elements.
The meter reading was taken from a larger piece of bright metal substituted for the subject.

114

Below left:
As the diagram indicates, a sheet of or-
dinary double-thick window glass was
placed on sawhorses in front of a white
no-seam background. In this first-step
photograph, the only illumination was
provided by a spotlight placed close to
the background directly behind the glass
container.
A 240 mm. lens was used on the camera
in place of the usual 105 mm. lens to
minimize the distortion which would result from the protruding handle and spout.

Below right:
In the completed lighting setup, two
spotlights were placed at either side of
the subject. To the left was a spotlight
with a very small snoot whose only purpose was to light the left side of the cork.
From the right, another small spotlight
was directed on the cork stopper. Note
that the glass picked up a few small highlights from these two sources, even
though they were not directly lighting
the glass.

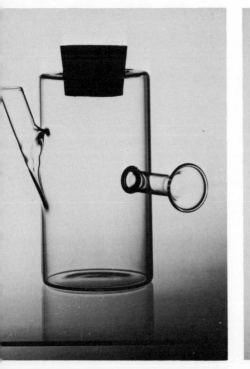

115

The crude finish and pressed design of this antique goblet tended to refract and diffuse the light within the glass much more readily than in the precise modern coffee pot. Showing the irregularities in this piece was important in cataloging it precisely.

The prime illumination was provided by a low-power baby spotlight directly beneath the goblet. Highlights in the embossed sections were brought up strongly by another spotlight directed on the goblet from the right.

This is a typical salesman's photograph. In black-and-white it would have to be supplemented by actual color samples. Note that three types of covers and a variety of shapes and sizes are shown. While descriptive, this type of photograph can hardly be considered as exciting as the color photograph of the same products which appears on page 35. In this case, obviously, color is badly needed.

Illumination was provided by two 500-watt lamps under a translucent light table and one 500-watt spotlight above and to the right of the subject. The use of the light table, highly illuminated, eliminated the shadows caused by the spotlight directed onto the subject.

Note that there is a degree of "falling off" to the left of the photo and a kind of distortion created by using a short lens (105 mm.) and working close to the subject. This distortion could have been corrected by substituting a longer lens and moving the camera back.

REFLECTIVE OBJECTS

In taking a picture of reflective objects you are, in a sense, not taking a picture of the object itself but rather of that which the object reflects. The shape of the object and the degree of reflectivity are prime determinants of the set-up required. If an object consists largely of flat planes, as in the case of the tin horse shown on the following page, the problem is simplified. We can visualize effect using the "billiard ball" approach to light; "the angle of incidence equals the angle of reflection." By placing a partial tent in front of, below, and behind the horse, all principle planes reflect even, illuminated surfaces. On the right edge of the base, an untented, darker area of the open end is reflected, but this is desirable as it separates that plane of the base.

The most difficult object to photograph is a highly polished spherical object, since it reflects everything around it. Such objects require a full tent, completely surrounding the object, with one hole poked through for the camera lens. In such cases, a translucent material must be used for the tent, since no lights can be placed inside the tent (they would be reflected in the object being photographed).

In a closed tent, a meter reading for exposure should be made before the tent is completely closed.

Left:
A simple tent with open ends was created of white no-seam paper. The translucent colors of the tin figure tended to matte the object, making it less critically reflective. In this case, lights can be directed from the outside to illuminate the inside of the tent.
Dulling sprays can be used on bright metal objects, acting in much the same way as the transparent paints on the horse. However, they completely obscure the true nature of the reflective material being photographed and should be limited to emergency use or record photography.

Opposite above:
When this spherical object was placed in the same tent as the horse figure, the dark areas beyond the edge of the tent obscured the shape. Lights are reflected in the object.

Opposite below:
As shown in the diagram a tent was constructed of white tracing tissue illuminated from the outside. While some variations in the fold and proximity of the tissue can be seen reflected in the sphere, there are no large black areas which will destroy the shape.
First the camera-subject relationship is set up; then the tent is built. If reflective objects are a significant part of your work, a permanent tent in your working space will save much time in construction and, after testing, can provide you with a uniform exposure. Temporary tents can be supported by string or wire, using transparent tape to attach the tissue.

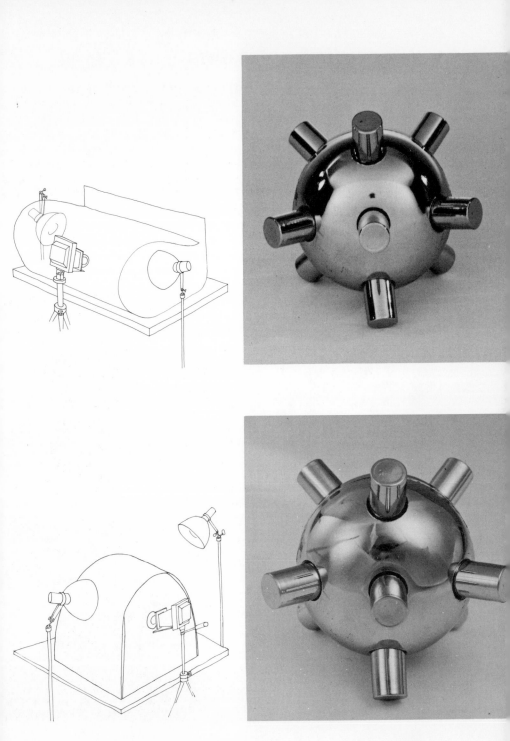

TWO-DIMENSIONAL OBJECTS

Most two-directional objects require flat lighting, distributed as evenly as possible. Reflectors, such as the Smith Victor flood reflectors pictured here, will provide a wide angle of balanced illumination. They should be placed at equal distances from the flat object being photographed and, as nearly as possible, at the same angle from the subject. Using the flat disk provided with most incident light meters, measure light falling on all parts of your subject and adjust your lights until illumination is perfectly even. If you are using a reflected light meter, check every part of the subject by reflected light, being careful not to pick up your own shadows.

In photographing paintings or other two dimensional subjects in which texture is not important, two wide-beam floodlights should be placed at an equal distance from the camera on either side. The camera should be centered on the subject, if possible. Overall illumination must be checked at all points on the subject with the light meter to insure that the light is perfectly balanced over the entire subject. If a large subject is being illuminated, diffusers over the floodlights can often help to produce more even illumination. Should texture be an important element of such a flat subject, you may wish to add a spotlight to one side to "brush" across the surface of the picture or tapestry being photographed. See color photograph page 38.

10.Consider the Background

Background generally occupies a significant portion of the picture area. It is by definition less important than the subject but it cannot be ignored, lest its effect be negative.

A background should be neutral and unnoticed or it should complement the idea and visual theme of the picture. In product photography the background is most often eliminated. A totally bland background can be produced with the use of no-seam paper. No-seam is smooth, matte paper available in rolls of white, black, several shades of gray, and many other colors. Widely used in display work, it can generally be purchased in display houses as well as professional photographic supply stores. Its name derives from the fact that it comes in very wide rolls — 107″ x 12 yards or 54″ x 12 yards are commonly available sizes.

Handling a no-seam roll takes a little practice and forethought. A roll can easily be carried by one person, but to hang it, an extra pair of hands helps. It creases easily, and every wrinkle will show under the lights. It should be taped or stapled to the panel or wall that forms the vertical background for your pictures. It must be rolled out carefully and evenly. A complete bottom and backdrop can be made in one sweep. Even ceilings of no-seam can be hung with the aid of a few long poles, a tacking stapler, and some extra light stands. Such reflective ceilings, especially when white no-seam is used, can be extremely helpful for bounce light setups when the ceiling of the space in which you are working is too high or insufficiently reflective. You are likely to use a colored no-seam background only for color work; a colored reflective ceiling or side drape would of course reflect colored light.

122

First, determine how high your background must reach. Pull the free end of the roll to the desired height, leaving the balance of the roll on the core. Tape or tack-staple the no-seam to the wall you are using as a background. Be sure it is firmly attached. If you are planning to shoot on the floor, simply roll the paper away from the wall, being careful not to make a corner where wall meets floor. Ideally, as the sweep of paper breaks from the wall to the floor, the sweep should describe a curve of paper with the radius of the curve being at least a foot. Then draw the paper forward as far as you believe you will need it.

If you have a subject suited to working at table height, you can use anything that will hold a raised platform as a table, since it will be covered by paper. A couple of boxes and a plywood sheet are adequate. (Be sure the table is steady enough not to move with slight vibrations of the floor.) The procedure for draping the paper sweep is the same except that it will be brought forward over the table surface and then down to the floor rather than directly down to the floor. Note that your table need not abut the wall.

If you are setting up a permanent studio, it can be a great timesaver to install permanently some rolls of paper in the colors you most commonly use. Purchase a long wood pole or pipe somewhat smaller in diameter than the inside of the core on which the no-seam paper comes rolled and about ten inches greater in length. This pole or pipe can then be positioned as high as possible on your studio wall and fixed to the wall by any sort of simple bracket that will allow both its free rotation and removal for reloading with paper. The paper can then be pulled down as needed and cut off from the bottom of the roll as it becomes soiled.

No-seam paper has a matte finish and soils easily. A damp, dirty hand, dirt on the bottom of an object placed on it, or walking on it will all dirty a no-seam surface. An artgum eraser will help clean up small marks, but not making any marks is better. The paper is cheap enough, but changing it can be a nuisance. If you must walk on a no-seam background, use cardboard as stepping stones or slip off your shoes.

One mistake frequently made when using seamless backgrounds is to put the object too close to the background. You have much greater lighting control if you leave four feet or more between the front of your subject and the background. This allows you to light the background independently of the subject without unwanted light spill either from it or from the subject onto it. The background can be hit with a spotlight to create a bright area in back of your subject or it can be cast into shadow providing an even flow of light to dark in the picture. If you are going to buy only one roll of no-seam, and I feel it is a must in any studio, buy white. Obviously, all colors will work against white. Even with white objects on white, you can control the relative illumination of the object and the background through lighting intensity, and thereby achieve satisfactory tonal separation. By controlling background illumination, you can obtain a wide range of light to deep gray tones on white.

Eastman Kodak produces, but does not market at retail, a material called Kodacel. While far more expensive than no-seam, it is a good deal more durable. Being translucent, lighting from behind this sheet material can cancel out multiple shadows resulting from the complex lighting arrangements occasionally needed for optimum product detail. Sources of this material are listed in Kodak's professional data book, *Studio Lighting*. Kodacel is available in rolls forty inches wide or in cut sheets.

Once the no-seam is set up, you can begin to introduce props to create a milieu for your subject. An intricately worked bracelet might call for just a touch of softness and a silk scarf might be introduced as a prop. A bough of holly and a punch bowl next to a glass might suggest Christmas. The idea of precision might be communicated graphically by placing calipers in a picture of a machined part. A beautifully bound book and an interesting pipe might evoke the quality of a box of tobacco. The trick is to suggest mood, use, or scale with props but definitely to subordinate them to the principal subject. Something as simple as a shadow cast on a no-seam background can be an effective prop.

Expressive or complementary backgrounds can be an interesting addition to a photograph. A pair of rough leather sandals shown against a weathered wood wall will emphasize the idea that the shoes are for country dress. A Mondrian-like print might well highlight an object of distinctly contemporary design. A highly polished (pull out your polarizing filter!) traditional wood table might add to the statement you would like to make about delicate chinaware. A package suggesting a masculine, outdoor character could well be pictured against a sea scene or rugged landscape. But be careful not to let the background dominate.

The shocking juxtaposition of normally discordant or unrelated elements can also be effective. A fuzzy slipper will never look softer than when you set it on an angular, polished steel sculpture. A bottle of champagne hung over the side of a disreputable rowboat to cool will arrest attention more surely than if it were placed in a silver chilling bucket. A delicate stemmed goblet photographed on rough cobblestones could be exciting. Such shock techniques would be more frequently used in advertising or poster work than in descriptive photography, but they are used in advertisements because they are interesting. Nobody ever said a presentation of any kind had to be dull and the possibilities are endless.

Outdoors, angle and focus are your tools for controlling background.

You can use depth of field selectively to keep your background out of focus. A low angle, which places your subject before the sky, or a very high shooting position in relation to your subject will often eliminate the things you do not want in your pictures. While you have limited lighting control out of doors, there are situations where you can place your subject in bright sunlight and shoot against a background of deep shade. Syncho-sunlight techniques (see Chapter 8) can also allow you to obtain proper foreground exposure for your subject while severely underexposing background elements. Often the right location and a few reflectors for minimum light control are all you will need.

Professionals, especially in advertising, think background so important that they will spend almost unlimited time and money to find the situation that says what they want to say about their product most forcefully. One of the classic examples is the sending of a top fashion photographer to Egypt to photograph a cold martini in front of the pyramids! The idea was that the particular brand of gin used was dry. While flying to Egypt might be impractical for most of us, there are a lot of possibilities for making photographs where we are. Start to collect them visually. Try new approaches. Just remember what the objective of your photography is. Try to stay away from the tried and trite in your selection of the second most important element in your picture, the background.

11. Preparing for the Printer

Most of the photographs we see each day, with the exception of film footage seen on t.v., are printed. Photographs that come to us in catalogs, newspapers, and magazines have been reproduced by photomechanical means. The preparation of photographs for photomechanical reproduction differs somewhat from shooting for photographic printing. Then, too, some knowledge of the related non-photographic problems of producing printed material should be helpful if you are considering the preparation of catalogs, brochures, illustrated programs, or mailing pieces.

While there are other methods of printing, we shall concern ourselves with the method called photo offset. It is not only the most suitable means of producing relatively short runs of printed material, but it will reproduce on almost any paper stock, offers the possibility of fine-quality reproduction in both color and black-and-white, and is generally available.

A good printer's objective is to reproduce photographs and other art he is given as accurately as possible. He looks first for sharpness, whether in color or black-and-white. He thinks of his work, as you should, in terms of optimum clarity. This is especially true when products are being illustrated.

Ideally, you should give the printer photographic prints or transparencies the same size as the finished work you want him to produce. He can pick up some sharpness by reducing from the print or transparency you give him; however, reduction should be held within limits of perhaps 25 to 30 percent (linear measurement). If he tries to reduce too much, middle tones will be lost; sharp detail will tend to clump, and contrast will build up. While the printer can also enlarge when he makes his halftone plates, this results in some loss of sharpness and should be avoided when possible or limited to the same 25 or 30 percent.

If you are using small photographs that require the reproduction of significant fine detail in your catalog, you will want to employ a printer who can use a fine screen, perhaps as fine as 200 lines per inch. Printing with a fine screen requires a precision printing press. Many printers cannot handle such work economically. Their presses are perhaps tuned to only 70 percent or 80 percent of the maximum precision obtainable. Presses can be adjusted to close to 100 percent accuracy, but they must be adjusted by skilled craftsmen frequently and carefully. This is one reason that the work of a fine printer costs more. The local printer who produces the local weekly newspaper for his prime income is not required to achieve top illustrative quality and consequently can get adequate results with less exacting press adjustment. He is not likely to change his habits to produce one work of art.

Contrast is, perhaps, the next quality noticed in a printed photograph. In a black-and-white photograph you start with clear negative material capable of reproducing a density range of about 200 to 1 (as measured by a densitometer). The photographic print you make, depending on the type, offers an optimum density range of less than 100 to 1. Quality printing can handle a contrast range of only about 40 to 1. Therefore, when you are photographing, you should light for a maximum density range of about 40 to 1. Light to bring the extremes of highlights and shadow closer together than you would shooting for photographic printing. The printer will lose about 10 percent of the tonal range at both the top and bottom of the density scale when he prints your photograph. A sparkling print with a full tonal range will, naturally, give him a chance to make a printed page of good tonality. As all of us who have looked at a printed photograph through a magnifier know, the printer does not print a solid mass of tone. He breaks up either tones or colors into dots, and this results in some loss of definition.

The printer must rephotograph your photograph to make his plates, so it is easily understood that reflections from the surface of your print may create problems for him. While printers will accept glossies for fine reproduction, they prefer matte prints. If a print is glossy, the gloss, produced by drying on a ferrotyping tin, should be absolutely even. This is a very difficult thing for any but a professional photographic laboratory to accomplish with regularity. Matte prints are easier and safer. Certainly, if there is any retouching to be done, you will want your prints on matte stock. Obviously, prints must be clean. The printer's camera picks up what is there, including dirt and defects. Spotting or retouching can sometimes save a bad print, but for critical work retouching should be handled by a good professional.

COLOR REPRODUCTION

Printers should be given color transparencies. It is more expensive and far less satisfactory to reproduce from color prints. Only as an emergency measure can reproduction be done from a color print. However, black-and-white reproductions are easily made from color prints.

In general, color reproduction makes the same demands of the photographer as black-and-white reproduction. Sharpness, controlled contrast, and other qualities of a good black-and-white photograph are just as important in a transparency. But while some adjustment in contrast can be effected by the printer with black-and-white film, his ability to correct contrast in color work is very limited. He can do some color correction in printing, but this too is limited and the original material which you furnish him should resemble as closely as possible the result you expect from him.

The same rule as to size applies in color as in black-and-white. A near-perfect 35 mm. transparency can be enlarged by a top printer up to thirty-five times, perhaps, but it is a painstaking job and very expensive. If one is going to depart from the 1:1 size ratio, it is better to require reduction or a minimum of enlargement.

SCALING OF PHOTOGRAPHS

Let us assume the printed piece you wish to produce will have a dozen photographic illustrations. Let us further assume that these illustrations will appear in two different final sizes in a catalog. One group will be 4″ x 5″ and the others will be printed as 2″ x 2½″. There will be six of each size. You will save a significant amount of money if the printer can shoot six, or, depending on the size of the work and his equipment, even twelve halftones on one halftone negative or, in the case of color film, make one color separation of six or twelve transparencies at once. To do so, he needs prints from you that are printed in scale. This means that your photographic prints must be 4″ x 5″ or proportioned to 4″ x 5″, say 6″ x 7½″. If you wanted to have him shoot the 2″ x 2½″ images at the same time, these would have to be proportioned as a group and also proportioned to the larger images. Using 6″ x 7½″ above for the work you wish to have reproduced on the printed page as 4″ x 5″, then the smaller prints would have to be given to the printer similarly 50 percent larger than you expect them to appear, or 3″ x 3¾″. Obviously if you are willing to print to scale or to actual size, which is fairly easily done with an enlarger, you could give him twelve different-sized prints to be mounted and rephotographed at one time and to be reproduced as twelve different sizes.

A layout of the printed page, even a rough sketch, should be prepared in advance. You should then shoot to layout sizes. If you are using a larger-format camera with a ground-glass focusing panel, you can predetermine size and mark the area to be included in the finished work right on the groundglass with a china marking pencil. Your scaling to size can then take place when you first make the negative. This can be especially helpful in color work where you cannot adjust the size of the transparency in a print. While much more difficult with a small negative, some approximation of size can be attempted in the camera and the slide can be masked with tape after processing.

THE PRINTING OF COLOR

In printing, black-and-white material is considered one color. The one color could be any color, of course, and except for the makeready time the printer would have to charge you for a special color of ink, it would be just like printing in black. Many jobs are done in two colors. These are generally one color plus black. Three-color printing is less often seen, since it closely approaches a full-color print in cost. While there are some three-color "full-color" processes, quality full-color work generally means four colors.

Each color increases your cost. While there are highly sophisticated presses which print two colors by making two separate passes at the sheet, and even full color by making four passes, each different color usually means a separate printing. In effect, the paper must be run through the press another time for each color. This will be especially true if you are making a short run (under 10,000 pieces) with a small printer. Consequently, each additional color costs almost as much in printing time, plates, makeready, and cleanup as another one-color job. Two colors cost nearly twice what a single color costs. Three colors cost nearly three times as much. The cost of paper does not, of course, increase.

Four colors means full color. While in printing less than full-color work your printer may have to mix ink to a desired color, in full-color work he always prints in dots of primary colors — yellow, cyan blue, magenta and black. Good offset color can produce almost any hue.

LAYOUT

If you are going to attempt to design or lay out your own printed material, some familiarity with a number of nonphotographic problems will be helpful. The making of a mechanical or pasteup is a skilled job. The mechanical is a board on which type and/or artwork and photographs are positioned and scaled, ready for the printer's camera. Unless you are actually trained in such work, it is better left to a professional.

First, line art — that is, illustrations or type as distinguished from halftones — must be pasted up and stripped in separately from photographs or other materials containing halftones. You can combine line drawings (preferably in dense black ink on white stock) with type on a single mechanical. Halftone art requires a mechanical which is prepared separately and printed in register with the line art work.

Sheet size is a prime consideration. Printed books were originally standard in a size of 6″ x 9″, and the standard printing paper sheet developed as a multiple of four book pages and became 25″ x 38″. The extra one inch in width and two inches in length of a standard sheet allows for gripping edges and trimming in binding. Today, paper can also be bought cut to produce 8½″ x 11″ pages. A 22½″ x 35″ sheet may be used for this size. If you want a

7" x 10" finished page, your printer might buy stock in a 22" x 28" sheet for you. Not only paper, but the presses that print them, are geared to such standard sizes, and an early conference with your printer to determine an economical page size is a good precaution before beginning to design your piece.

A word should be said about paper quality. In limited runs, the cost of paper is a relatively small part of the total printing job. For the few extra dollars, choosing the best-quality paper suitable to your job will pay off in better detail and visual effectiveness. Accept your printer's advice.

Typesetting is the next most important consideration. There are several ways of preparing your verbal message. A new and relatively inexpensive method of obtaining written copy is through the use of a special IBM typewriter designed for this purpose. This machine can produce justified margins (margins which are straight up and down on both sides) and offer a good, if rather limited, selection of type faces. They can produce excellent, clear copy. The local IBM office can probably tell you where you can obtain such service.

Another budget method of setting is VariType. VariType can be half the price of even an inexpensive typesetting job, but it is visually distinguishable. Not only is it less regular (spacing between letters is not as even as typesetting), but it offers a rather limited selection of type faces and sizes to begin with. Unless you are planning to produce a very inexpensive piece and do not mind if it looks inexpensive, it is worthwhile to pay the extra cost of typesetting. This is especially true if your design calls for justified margins, since the VariTyper must do the copy twice to produce such margins, and the cost about doubles.

Most quality work is still the result of a typesetter's hand, and typesetting is an art. You can choose, depending on what your printer has available, from a very wide variety of faces and sizes. When you look at a well-set page, you will see an evenness of pattern, without vertical "rivers" of white space. Each letter will be free of voids, and each letter on the page will be as dense and clean as the others. You can spot poor typesetting by the lack of these qualities as well as by squashed type impressions in which the letters lack clarity and may even show breaks. Typesetting varies tremendously in cost. As in choosing a printer, select a typesetter by the quality of his sample work. Better yet, let your printer deal with a typesetter and be responsible for the overall job. He will get a trade price from a type house; alone you will be likely to have to pay an agency price or more.

The typesetter does not usually provide you with a fully set page, although he can. In catalog work, he will provide you with blocks of printed type, which you can then cut and paste in position on your layout.

If you plan to do a tight design, you will have to specify type face and size and then scale it on your layout so that it can be pasted in on the mechanical. To do this, in addition to some experience, you will need a type book. Sample books are prepared by typographers as catalogs of available type faces and sizes. An examination of sample pages will help you to determine what face and size you wish to use in a given space. Your printer should have such type books available for loan to you from the typographers with whom he does business. A tentative selection of type face and size will help you adjust your layout, even if roughly, and will show you how much space your copy will occupy. Therefore, even if you plan to use the services of a professional graphic artist for the final work, or let your printer do it, a review of typographic possibilities in advance will help you to make your rough layout for photography more realistic.

BINDING

Binding is an important consideration. If you have a simple folded sheet, binding is not a problem, but if the material is over four pages, it generally will have to be bound. From a design point of view, the final method of binding should be considered at the time you are preparing your material. There are relatively few popular methods for most catalogs or other thin books.

First, you must print in "forms" of four, eight, sixteen, or thirty-two pages, or combinations thereof. You cannot bind a nine- or seventeen-page book, at least not economically. A four-page form folded in the middle and printed on two sides, is actually two pages. For example, a four-page form producing 6" x 9" pages and bound vertically would be a sheet 12" x 9" printed on both sides. Since a larger form is printed on a larger press in a single impression, it is more economical than a combination of smaller ones to produce a given number of pages.

Saddle-stitch binding is the most popular for short catalog runs of books of up to thirty-two or even forty-eight pages. This method can be recognized by the staples that are driven through the fold of the book. It is inexpensive, generally available, and quite clean looking.

Another method, Perfect binding, is growing in popularity. For runs of perhaps 5,000 or more, this glue-binding method can work very well. It requires a separate cover and the edges of the pages are glued to that cover. It is essentially the way a cheap note pad is bound. Perfect binding allows great versatility in the number of pages and type of insertion. It, too, is relatively inexpensive.

Smythe-sewn binding is generally used in more expensive publications with a great number of pages. When a book is to be used repeatedly, as a reference, for example, this method might well be used. Its advantage is primarily that forms of different numbers of pages, each sewn together, can then be bound into a single cover. Further, a Smythe-sewn book will lie nearly flat when open. While certainly not a catalog technique, you may need to use it for other publications.

The looseleaf method of collating sheets into some outer folder or binder is flexible, and for this reason sometimes appealing. Its seductiveness generally derives from the idea that the recipient of the folder of sheets can subsequently be sent additions and be asked to withdraw sheets. In fact, I know of few people or firms that ever follow up with additional sheets, and I believe there are fewer recipients who delete and add sheets as the sender would like him to do. While the sheets are generally cheaper than a bound book, the cover or envelope into which they are placed usually far exceeds any known binding method in cost. Think twice before using this method.

Plastic comb and wire spiral bindings can be very handsome, but unless your run of a publication is very small, they are very expensive. The insertion of a plastic comb is hand work, and it can run ten to twenty cents per copy for normal catalog size. Wire binding is less, but still far more costly than other methods discussed above.

One creative possibility in binding, which is often not exploited, and which can be used without great cost, is the mixing of different paper stocks within one book. Each form being a minimum of four pages, it is easy to see that each one could be printed on a different paper and then bound together. Even a little sixteen page book might use, for example, eight pages of a clear white matte stock for photograph and type presentation and another eight-page form printed on a gray, textured stock to carry editorial copy and/or drawings. The gray stock might even be handled in such a way as to provide an interesting self-cover. Depending on the effect you want, this might be something to explore with your printer.

There are few commodities to be bought where the cost for a given job is so directly related to visible quality as in printing. I am not suggesting that only the best will do, but the buyer of printing must realize that, in a given market, lower price means lower quality. The quality of graphic reproduction, typesetting, binding, and paper stock all enter into this final cost. One should try to buy at a quality-level adequate to one's purpose. An honest printer with a good reputation, like most businessmen, will help a new customer to make the right choices.

I qualify cost as being "in a given market" because two different metropolitan areas may well offer a significant differential in printing prices. Printing costs are largely labor. In a town with a strong printing union, prices may be substantially higher than in a neighboring, less organized area. Checking with businesses that buy printing in your community may well save you money.

The printer with whom you work will initially be educating you. Work closely with him. Show him your first photographs to find out if you will be giving him what he needs. Submit your layouts as suggestions. From his requests and criticisms in trying to get your first few printing jobs "to bed," you will learn more than any text can possibly teach you. If you become involved in your own printing preparation, the education your printer will give you may well be worth more than the finished job.

Appendix A

INSTRUCTING THE LABORATORY

When a custom laboratory develops your film or makes your enlargements, you can expect and generally get a certain amount of personal attention to your work. You must, however, tell the lab what you want done.

Developing Your Film
The laboratory can compensate for changes in exposure to a considerable degree. While "forcing" film for higher speed results in grainier negatives, it can also increase subject contrast. Thus, a film (black-and-white) rated at A.S.A. 80 can be exposed at a 50 percent speed increase or A.S.A. 120 (increases of over 50 percent are chancy). If you mark your roll with the A.S.A. speed at which it was exposed, the lab will compensate by increasing development time.

Similarly, if you are dealing with an extremely contrasty subject and wish to reduce contrast, you can cut the speed of your film by giving it longer exposure, and the lab can reduce the developing time. Again, a 50 percent limit is advisable.

Making Your Enlargements
A generally recognized code is used by most professional laboratories to indicate to the printer what you want done. You can mark a contact print using this code and attach it to your negative for the printer to follow. These are the most common indicators you will employ:

For burning in, or making an area of a print darker, use crosshatch lines over the area you wish to have darkened.

To indicate dodging, or making an area lighter, mark the area on your contact proof or proof print with small circles.

When accurate cropping is desired, especially if you do not wish the lab to print on a full sheet of standard paper, use straight lines to indicate the edges of your picture. When cropping is to be approximate, use wiggly lines to indicate that the picture will print on standard sheet sizes, approximately as you have indicated.

Common-sense instructions eliminate errors. Such instructions as "print full negative," "full paper size," "crop to subject," "crop to central element of subject: see contact print," etc., will also be understood.

Appendix B

PROFESSIONAL LABORATORIES

Probably there is a custom laboratory somewhere in your area that can develop and print black-and-white photographs to your satisfaction. A professional photographer or your local professional photographic supply store can probably tell you where such services exist nearby. Since the prices, compared to mass finishing, are likely to seem very high, I quote some typical current New York prices*:

develop and print 120 or 35mm. film and provide contact proof sheet	$2.50 roll
4" x 5" cut film, developing only	$3.60 doz.
1—2 enlargements from same negative 8" x 10"	$2.00
11" x 14"	$3.00
16" x 20"	$6.00

Other typical lab services include dry mounting, numbering of negatives, and salon printmaking. In addition, many provide color processing and printing services.

Should you be working in an area where good photographic services are not available, the following New York laboratories are all excellent and will work by mail.

    Bernard Hoffman Laboratories, 222 East 44th Street, (10017)
    Leco Photo Service, Inc., 1 East 42 Street ,(10017)
    Modern Age Photographic Services, Inc., 319 East 44th Street, (10017)

Write to them for instructions and price lists if you lack a satisfactory local laboratory. Best of all, learn to do your darkroom work yourself.

* Prices courtesy Modern Age, N.Y.C.

CLOSEUP EXPOSURE CALCULATIONS

When photographing small objects, you will wish to fill your negative. This is generally accomplished by moving the camera closer to the subject. To bring a close object into focus, you must extend your lens through the use of a bellows, extension tubes, or similar devices that increase the lens-to-film distance.

As a practical matter, *when the subject is closer than eight times the focal length of the lens you are using, you must calculate for increased exposure time.* The f-stops are no longer accurate indicators of lens speed. Therefore, for example, if you are using a 6″ (150mm.) lens and your lens-to-subject distance is less than 48″, you will have to recalculate exposure. This is especially critical with color films which have a very limited margin for error in exposure.

The easiest way to do this without guides and table is to match, with a simple ruler, the image size (size of the object being photographed on the ground glass of the camera) to the actual size of the object being photographed. This will give you your magnification ratio. For example, if you are photographing an object 4″ tall which measures 2″ tall on your ground glass, you have an image-subject magnification ratio of 2/4, or .5. If the image on the ground glass is 4″ and the subject 2″, your ratio would be 4/2, or 2. This magnification ratio is indicated in the following formula as M.

The simple formula for computing exposure-time increase is:

$(M+1)^2$ = exposure factor

Thus, if your image/subject magnification ratio is $^1/_2$, you would use $^1/_2$ in the formula as follows:

$(^1/_2+1)^2$ becomes $(1^1/_2)^2$ or $2^1/_4$ (exposure factor)

In this example, if your exposure meter indicated an exposure time of 1 second at a given f-stop, you would increase exposure $2^1/_4$ times, or use an exposure of $2^1/_4$ seconds.

Similarly, if your magnification ratio were 2/1, M would equal 2, and the formula would work as follows:

$(2+1)^2$ becomes $(3)^2$ or 9 (exposure factor)

Your 1-second exposure would then become 9 seconds.

If, on the other hand, you wish to vary the f-stop, or lens opening, rather than the exposure time, you can do so by using the same formula without squaring it and dividing the result into the f-stop.

$$\frac{f\text{-stop}}{(M+1)}$$

For example, let us assume your normal f-stop indicated by your meter is f/16. You have determined that M (magnification of image/subject size) is 2, then:

$$\frac{f/16}{2+1} = \frac{f/16}{3} = f/5.3$$

You keep the exposure time constant as indicated by your meter, but open your lens to f/5.3 (in practical terms, a little above f/5.6).

If your photograph requires keeping depth of field, you will wish to retain a small f-stop and increase exposure time. Use the $(M+1)^2$ formula.

If you wish to keep your exposure short (because of possible camera or subject movement or because exposure would exceed the recommended length of exposure of a color film), increase the lens opening by the factor indicated in the $(M+1)$ formula.

Appendix D

RECOMMENDED TYPES OF LIGHTING EQUIPMENT FOR OCCASIONAL STUDIO USE

1. This type of stamped steel reflector is basic to studio lighting. Sturdy position-locks and porcelain sockets will save much frustration. Various widths of light beams are available. For close working quarters, choose wide-beam reflectors. When more comfortable shooting quarters are available, choose a narrower light beam to afford greater light-to-subject distances. Reflectors of this type are commonly referred to as flood lamps.

2. Quartz lamps offer great advantages of steady color temperature, long bulb-life, and ease in packing and carrying. Unfortunately, most models do not yet allow the degree of light-control that can be obtained with conventional flood- and spotlighting.

3. Reflectors equipped with diffusion screens produce a softer, more even light than reflectors without them. They also tend to eliminate "hot spots" in closeup lighting. The commercial models are most handy. You can, however, substitute sheets of white tracing paper with two or three wood clothespins to hold the paper over the flood lamp reflector.

4. Barn doors are a basic lighting-control tool. They can be opened wide or closed to a slit to allow a narrow beam of light to fall on your subject. They can eliminate light on backgrounds and in other areas of the picture where light spill is undesirable. It is preferable to equip every flood reflector with them and leave them in place. Although cardboard sheets and tape can substitute for commercial barn doors in an emergency, commercial models are recommended.

1. Model AP18, Studio Light

2. Model QI-P, Quartz Light

3. Model DP, Diffusion Screens

4. Model BD, Barndoors

135

5. Model SA, Stand

5. Model S3, Stand

6. Model 851, Stand

7. "Baby" Spot, Type 751

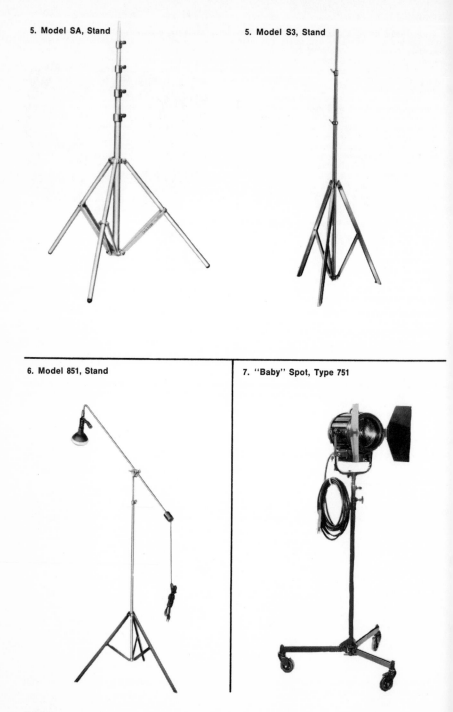

136

5. These stands are typical of many folding types available. Steel units, such as that shown at the right, are inexpensive and sturdy but lack the easy portability of the multi-section aluminum models. Check the "bargain models" for ease of working all parts. Avoid light, brittle cast-metal joints. Be sure they are sturdy enough to hold the lights you want to use with them.

6. A simple boom arm mounted on a portable stand will allow you to put floodlights and spots exactly where you want them, including directly over a subject. A couple of these can be a big help in solving lighting problems.

7. Two or more matched spotlights plus a "baby" spot can give you nearly complete control of lighting. Generally, a 1000-watt unit will handle most table-top or product needs, and if you consistently work with small objects under 18" in maximum dimension, 500-watt units will suffice. Unfortunately, the lenses, heatproof construction, and polished mirrors needed for a good spotlight are expensive. The "amateur" 500-watt and 1000-watt units are generally inefficient in comparison with professional equipment and may prove less than satisfactory. This model is by Mole-Richardson Co. Note the sturdy rolling stand.

All lighting equipment shown here is available from Smith-Victor Corp., Griffith, Indiana 46319, except as noted. This company's Professional line offers excellent products at reasonable prices.

Appendix E

FILTERS FOR COLOR PHOTOGRAPHY

If you can use a film balanced for the color temperature of your source, there is no need to employ color filters. However, because of your demand for a certain film speed or other characteristics, you may have to use films not exactly suited to the lights you employ. Furthermore, some special effect or an exceptionally critical demand for nearly perfect color accuracy may lead you to use filtration.

To expose color film designed for one type of illumination under a light source of different color temperature, you must employ conversion filters.

Standard conversion filters will generally suffice to balance a light source of a given color temperature to a film designed for illumination of a different color temperature; however, to create mood or induce a warmer or colder feeling in your colors, you may wish to employ light balancing filters. These do essentially the same thing as conversion filters but are produced in many more gradations of color for more accurate and selective control.

Note that while several filters may be combined for cumulative effect, the use of more than three will probably affect clarity.

For the most critical color photography, it may be necessary to employ color-compensating filters. Such filters may be required in very exacting color work to correct slight variations in film emulsion characteristics beyond the normal control of a manufacturer. Refer to the film manufacturer's data sheets and manuals for further information.

KODAK LIGHT BALANCING FILTERS

Reproduced with permission from *Kodak Color Films*, Kodak Publication No. E-77, 5th ed., 1968.

Color	WRATTEN Number	Exposure Increase in Stops*	Color Temperature of Source	
			Converted to 3200 K	Converted to 3400 K
Bluish	82C + 82C	$1^1/_3$	2490 K	2610 K
	82C + 82B	$1^1/_3$	2570 K	2700 K
	82C + 82A	1	2650 K	2780 K
	82C + 82	1	2720 K	2870 K
	82C	$^2/_3$	2800 K	2950 K
	82B	$^2/_3$	2900 K	3060 K
	82A	$^1/_3$	3000 K	3180 K
	82	$^1/_3$	3100 K	3290 K
No Filter Necessary			3200 K	3400 K
Yellowish	81	$^1/_3$	3300 K	3510 K
	81A	$^1/_3$	3400 K	3630 K
	81B	$^1/_3$	3500 K	3740 K
	81C	$^1/_3$	3600 K	3850 K
	81D	$^2/_3$	3700 K	3970 K
	81EF	$^2/_3$	3850 K	4140 K

*These values are approximate. For critical work, they should be checked by practical test, especially if more than one filter is used.

KODAK CONVERSION FILTERS

To Convert	Use KODAK Filter No.	Filter Color	Exposure Increase in Stops*
3200 K to Daylight (5500 K)	80A	Blue	2
3400 K to Daylight (5500 K)	80B	Blue	$1^2/_3$
3800K † to Daylight (5500 K)	80C	Blue	1
4200 ‡ to Daylight (5500 K)	80D	Blue	$^1/_3$
Daylight (5500 K) to 3800 K	85C	Orange	$^1/_3$
Daylight (5500 K) to 3400 K	85	Orange	$^2/_3$
Daylight (5500 K) to 3200 K	85B	Orange	$^2/_3$

* For critical work, check these values by practical test.
† Aluminum-filled clear flashbulbs, such as M2, 5, and 25.
‡ Zirconium-filled clear flashbulbs, such as AG-1, M3, and M5.

Appendix F

SAMPLE MODEL RELEASE FORM

Date_____

To: (your name)
    (your address)

Gentlemen:

I grant to you (and your assigns) the right to use and publish my photograph or likeness in catalogs, publicity, advertising, and for any other purpose. I desire to see that use and publication. I make this grant on the understanding that you will rely on it, and I waive and release you from all claims I may have on account of your use of this grant.

If I am a minor, this grant and release shall not be valid unless my parent or guardian shall execute the agreement below.

Very truly yours,

_____(Name)
_____(Address)

I am a parent/guardian of the above minor, and also desiring to see the above use and publication and understanding you will rely on the above grant and my agreement, I hereby agree that such minor and I will be bound by all the above terms.

_____(Name)
_____(Address)

BIBLIOGRAPHY

Because of changes in techniques, tools, and materials, much information that is available on the library shelves is outdated very quickly. The reading materials listed below have been updated recently or are the standard reference works of their kind. The books on photographic technique are without number! The following books and pamphlets have proved particularly helpful to me as a still-life photographer working with products. They offer specific information on special, often-encountered problems that could not be included in this volume.

ART

Robert E. Mates. *Photographing Art*. Philadelphia: Chilton Book Co.

BASIC PHOTOGRAPHY

How to Make Good Pictures. Rochester, N.Y.: Eastman Kodak Co. Covers basic snapshot problems but offers in any easy-to-read, easier-to-understand way an introduction to the principles of photography. Elementary.
Feininger, Andreas. *Successful Photography*. Englewood, N.J.: Prentice-Hall, Inc. A complete manual of the basics of picture-making and elementary darkroom technique. Very clearly written and well illustrated. As a nontechnical discussion of why things happen, photographically, it is an eminently readable first book for the serious beginner.

COLOR

Applied Color Photography Indoors. Rochester, N.Y.: Eastman Kodak Co., 1962. A well-illustrated pamphlet covering lighting sources and problems, backgrounds, and exposure factors in color work when performed under artificial light.
Feininger, Andreas. *Successful Color Photography*. Englewood, N.J.: Prentice-Hall, Inc., 1967. Treats color as a separate medium. Examines the nature of color photography, print types, basic materials, and equipment. Good early reading in color.

DARKROOM WORK

Lootens, J.B. *Lootens on Photographic Enlarging and Print Quality*. Philadelphia: Chilton Book Co., 7th ed., 1967. The bible of serious photographic printing. Updated materials and processes. A book dedicated to print quality.
Photolab Design. Rochester, N.Y.: Eastman Kodak Co. While oriented toward the professional, there is a good deal of thought-provoking information for the serious amateur.
Professional Printing in Black-and-White. Rochester, N.Y.: Eastman Kodak Co., 1970. A directly written instruction manual on printing. Concise and informative. Tells "tricks" of the trade.

FILTERS

Filters. Rochester, N.Y.: Eastman Kodak Co., 1965. A basic guide to the use of filters in both black-and-white and color photography. Good reference tables. Excellent hints for commercial product photography.

LIGHTING

Adams, Ansel. *Artificial Light Photography*. Hastings-on-the-Hudson, N.Y.: Morgan & Morgan, Inc. One of the masters discusses the technical and aesthetic aspects of photography without sunlight. Slow, technical reading at times, but well worth the trouble.
Nurnberg, Walter. *Lighting for Photography*. Philadelphia: Chilton Book Co., 16th ed., 1968. Relates properties of light to photographic materials for both black-and-white and color work. Excellent discussion of the principles of using multiple lights. For the still-life photographer, offers excellent discussions of problems related to different materials and textures.
Studio Lighting for Product Photography. Rochester, N.Y.: Eastman Kodak Co. An easy-to-follow and very well illustrated handbook covering, in detail, dozens of typical product-lighting problems encountered in commercial photography. While written for the fully equipped studio worker, it has a good deal of information for the at-home photographer of products.

MATERIALS

Kodak Color Films. Kodak Publication No. E-77, 5th ed., Rochester, N.Y.: Eastman Kodak Co., 1968
Kodak Black-and-White Films in Rolls. Kodak Publication No. AF 13. Rochester, N.Y.: Eastman Kodak Co.
Kodak Black-and-White Sheet Films. Kodak Publication No. F 5. Rochester, N.Y.: Eastman Kodak Co.
The editors of Eastman Kodak have compiled, in simple texts, almost everything you would have to know about exposing and processing their products. These are basic reference guides to keep at hand.

RETOUCHING

O.R. Croy. *Retouching.* London: Focal Press, 1964. It is always easier to retake than retouch, but when you can't retake a photograph, this guide to all types of retouching may help you to save or improve a picture.

VIEW-CAMERA TECHNIQUE

Camera Technique for Professional Photographers. Rochester, N.Y. Eastman Kodak Co., 1962. Probably the best book of its type for nonprofessionals as well. A complete handbook for the use of the view camera. All technical points of importance are covered. All commonly used reference information is included. Explains lenses in detail. Shows how to use the adjustments of a flexible camera. Solutions for distortion problems are included.

INDEX

142